NEW DIRECTIONS FOR COMMUNITY COLLEGES

Arthur M. Cohen
EDITOR-IN-CHIEF

Florence B. Brawer
ASSOCIATE EDITOR

School-to-Work Systems: The Role of Community Colleges in Preparing Students and Facilitating Transitions

Edgar I. Farmer
Pennsylvania State University

Cassy B. Key
Capital Area Tech-Prep/School-to-Work Consortium

EDITORS

Number 97, Spring 1997

JOSSEY-BASS PUBLISHERS
San Francisco

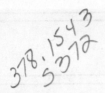

378.1543
5372

ERIC®
Clearinghouse for Community Colleges

SCHOOL-TO-WORK SYSTEMS: THE ROLE OF COMMUNITY COLLEGES IN
PREPARING STUDENTS AND FACILITATING TRANSITIONS
Edgar I. Farmer, Cassy B. Key (eds.)
New Directions for Community Colleges, no. 97
Volume XXV, number 1
Arthur M. Cohen, Editor-in-Chief
Florence B. Brawer, Associate Editor

Microfilm copies of issues and articles are available in 16mm and 35mm,
as well as microfiche in 105mm, through University Microfilms Inc.,
300 North Zeeb Road, Ann Arbor, Michigan 48106-1346.

ISSN 0194-3081   ISBN 0-7879-9817-6

NEW DIRECTIONS FOR COMMUNITY COLLEGES is part of The Jossey-Bass
Higher and Adult Education Series and is published quarterly by Jossey-
Bass Inc., Publishers, 350 Sansome Street, San Francisco, California
94104-1342, in association with the ERIC Clearinghouse for Community
Colleges. Periodicals postage paid at San Francisco, California, and at
additional mailing offices. POSTMASTER: Send address changes to New
Directions for Community Colleges, Jossey-Bass Inc., Publishers, 350
Sansome Street, San Francisco, California 94104-1342.

SUBSCRIPTIONS cost $53.00 for individuals and $89.00 for institutions,
agencies, and libraries. Prices subject to change.

THE MATERIAL in this publication is based on work sponsored wholly or
in part by the Office of Educational Research and Improvement, U.S.
Department of Education, under contract number RI-93-00-2003. Its con-
tents do not necessarily reflect the views of the Department or any other
agency of the U.S. Government.

EDITORIAL CORRESPONDENCE should be sent to the Editor-in-Chief, Arthur
M. Cohen, at the ERIC Clearinghouse for Community Colleges, Univer-
sity of California, 3051 Moore Hall, 405 Hilgard Avenue, Los Angeles,
California 90024-1521.

Cover photograph © Rene Sheret, After Image, Los Angeles, California, 1990.

Manufactured in the United States of America on Lyons Falls
TCF Pathfinder Tradebook. This paper is acid-free and 100 percent
totally chlorine-free.

Contents

EDITORS' NOTES

In the coming decades community colleges will prepare young people with academic and technical skills for entry-level employment in the global workplace. George Vaughan's 1995 work *The Community College Story: A Tale of American Innovation* reinforces the editors' position that community colleges are in the best position to play a major role in supporting consortia and training and retraining workers for the school-to-work system. The impact of community colleges on the lives of individuals and their communities, according to Vaughan, leaves little doubt about their leadership role in their respective service areas.

The statistics alone are impressive. Currently, there are 1,472 public community colleges, technical colleges, two-year branch colleges, and independent junior colleges in America, with an enrollment of over 5.7 million students in credit courses and millions more in noncredit courses, activities, and programs. (Vaughan, 1995). Based upon these statistics, the editors are convinced that community colleges will be the gateways for successful training and employment of the masses during the twenty-first century.

This practical sourcebook represents a collection of manuscripts from many noteworthy scholars, researchers, and practitioners in the school-to-work field and community college education. In Chapter One, Debra Bragg and Mildred Griggs set the tone for the sourcebook by discussing several important questions regarding the effectiveness of school-to-work systems. For example, what does research suggest about the status, prevalence, and success of school-based, work-based, and connecting components in community colleges? What is the history of their use there? And what is their future? The authors provide answers to these questions and more.

In Chapter Two, Margaret Ellibee and Sarah Mason examine the ways in which benchmarking, a continuous quality improvement process, can be used to define and improve the quality of school-to-work curricula. The authors contend that the benchmarking process, adapted from business and industry and labor, begins with self-study through the systematic review of established goals and objectives, followed by a self-assessment of existing practices and the collection of supporting information and data.

In Chapter Three, Mary Kisner, Maralyn Mazza, and David Liggett outline the steps to building partnerships between secondary and postsecondary educators and local businesses. The authors describe how to select strategic partners, how to set realistic goals, and how to maintain a partnership. In Chapter Four, David Just and Dewey Adams stress the importance of articulation for establishing a solid secondary and postsecondary link. The authors also discuss how community colleges are essential elements in strengthening the pathways between high school and higher education. The authors further describe several useful models for articulation with local high schools, community colleges, four-year colleges and universities, and industry training programs.

In Chapter Five, Laurel Adler details the role community colleges should play in developing effective job placement programs. Adler describes various partnership models where schools and community agencies work together to ensure that training actually results in job placements and also describes the interconnectedness between economic development and job training and placement.

In Chapter Six, Carl Price, Claudia Graham, and Janet Hobbs explain how to implement a workplace mentoring program for community college practitioners that includes identifying, recruiting, and selecting effective mentors as essential components of work-site learning strategies. The authors outline a series of steps in formulating mentoring programs as well as a generic model that depicts the four components of a successful workplace mentoring environment.

In Chapter Seven, Ann Doty and Robin Odom illustrate the attributes and characteristics of nine exemplary apprenticeship programs in community and technical colleges. These authors contend that apprenticeship programs should be custom-tailored to meet the business needs of the sponsoring employers and the career interests of the apprentice, as well as the approved apprenticeship standards of the registering agency.

In Chapter Eight, Joe Green and Phyllis Foley describe how community colleges are developing career awareness, career exploration, and decision-making skills in students. The authors explore new directions in community college curriculum development from the perspective of establishing hallmarks of quality initiatives. According to the authors, insistence on quality is critical in order to implement a "no-excuses" standard for delivery of quality products and services.

In Chapter Nine, Les Bolt and Ned Swartz discuss some of the major issues surrounding curriculum integration, with examples of how contextual learning models successfully integrate workplace skills into the curriculum.

In Chapter Ten, Donald Bryant and Mary Kirk describe some of the legal issues community colleges and employers face (as well as those of involved labor organizations). The authors raise several questions. For example, what is an institution's or company's legal liability for student apprentices and students in training? When is a learning experience, even though it might involve the performance of work, not considered employment? The authors contend that activities occurring in the workplace that do not involve the performance of work are not considered employment subject to the Fair Labor Standards Act.

In Chapter Eleven, we discuss the background and purpose of the School-to-Work Opportunities Act (STWOA) of 1994 and how the act should be administered for systemic effect. We also illuminate the three components involved in developing successful school-to-work systems, highlighting exemplary models for community college practitioners. One such model is tech-prep (technical preparation) programs, which demonstrate many of the same reform criteria as those suggested in the STWOA, including registered apprenticeships, curriculum development and integration, career development, and work-based learning programs.

Chapter Twelve concludes this sourcebook with an annotated bibliography of ERIC documents on school-to-work systems in community colleges and other two-year postsecondary institutions.

Edgar I. Farmer
Cassy B. Key
Editors

EDGAR I. FARMER is associate professor of workforce education and development at Pennsylvania State University.

CASSY B. KEY is executive director of the Capital Area Tech-Prep/School-to-Work Consortium in Austin, Texas.

Students in community colleges have acquired work-related learning experiences while pursuing postsecondary education. However, in most cases such learning experiences are neither well documented nor systematically monitored by the community colleges; they should be.

Assessing the Community College Role in School-to-Work Systems

Debra D. Bragg, Mildred Barnes Griggs

America's declining competitiveness is increasingly linked to inadequacies in human resources, including a lack of preparedness among entrants to the workforce (Marshall and Tucker, 1992; Reich, 1991, 1995). According to the Secretary's Commission on Achieving Necessary Skills (1991), too few new employees enter the labor market with the skills needed to fill jobs requiring technical sophistication. Often prospective workers are not ready or able to learn advanced academic or technical skills (Carnevale, Gainer, and Meltzer, 1990). Yet some of America's foreign competitors are preparing their people for the new economy and dealing effectively with contemporary workforce concerns. Technical training programs in several European countries use work-based learning systems that can and do facilitate the school-to-work transition (Nothdurft, 1989).

In Denmark and Germany, for example, the apprenticeship model is used to close the gap between school and work, with educators and employers sharing responsibility for work-based learning (Hamilton, 1990). The comparably high cost of work-based learning is shared by government and business; each of these entities perceives its contribution as an investment in the economic well-being of the country. In the United States, the situation differs significantly, with all but a few students—the small minority who are bound for four-year colleges or universities (the "college bound")—fending for themselves. Most youths receive little guidance in how to pursue further (postsecondary) education or work, and as a result some fail to make the transition from school to work altogether (Gray and Herr, 1995; Pennington, 1995).

Corson and Silverberg (1993) are among those who argue persuasively that the existing educational system is failing non-college-bound youth, limiting their potential to successfully make the transition from schooling to stable, high-wage employment: "America's emphasis on college preparation has isolated academic from vocational education and weakened schools' ability to prepare youths for the demands of employment. . . . Many youths, particularly those confronted with depressed local job markets and evidence that high school completion does not lead to rewarding employment, view the link between academia and successful employment as tenuous" (p. 3).

In recent years, concerns about gaps in student preparation for the school-to-work transition have been recognized widely, culminating in a new federal policy. The School-to-Work Opportunities Act (STWOA) of 1994 supports wide-scale application of work-based learning in the nation's systemic educational reform. The STWOA's primary goal is to establish a national framework to encourage states to coordinate state- and local-level school-to-work transition systems. These systems should be designed to help youths gain meaningful work experience while they are in school as well as identify and obtain rewarding work after completing secondary or postsecondary education.

Though no one model is endorsed by the STWOA, states and localities are encouraged to explore alternative approaches such as youth apprenticeships or tech-prep programs (Pennington, 1995; Reich, 1995). Successful completion of school-to-work programs is expected to result in a high school diploma, a certificate or degree from a postsecondary institution, or an occupational skill certificate (a portable, industry-recognized credential certifying competency and mastery of specific occupational skills). Regardless of the approach or model chosen, school-to-work transition systems should strengthen the relationships between academic and vocational education, educators and employers, and labor organizations and secondary and postsecondary education. And all three of these relationships need to be evident in the school-based learning, work-based learning, and connecting activity components of a school-to-work system.

The first component, school-based learning, involves career exploration and counseling, selection of a career-related major by grade 11, periodic evaluations linked to academic standards, and formal links between the secondary and postsecondary levels. The second component, work-based learning, involves paid or unpaid work experiences, workplace mentoring, and instruction in general workplace competencies as well as in all aspects of an industry. Connecting activities, the third component, are designed to ease the transition from in-school to out-of-school learning by matching students' interests and competencies to the work-based learning opportunities offered by employers. Career counseling, professional development of educators and workplace mentors, and job placement services are methods of facilitating the school-to-work transition.

Given the fundamental purpose and operational framework created by the STWOA, it is important to consider the role of community colleges in emerging school-to-work transition systems. What does research suggest about the status, prevalence, and success of school-based, work-based, and connecting components in community colleges? What is the history of their use there? What is their future? This chapter addresses these important questions, paying particular attention to what is known about the effectiveness of the triad of relationships existing between academic and vocational education, education and employers, and labor organizations and secondary and postsecondary education.

Assessing School-Based Learning in the Community College

Community colleges have a long and rich tradition of offering liberal arts–transfer and occupational-technical education programs for youths and adults (Cohen and Brawer, 1989). Particularly since the late 1960s and early 1970s, a primary function of all types of community colleges (including junior colleges and two-year postsecondary technical institutes) has been the delivery of occupational-technical education. Factors such as increased support for postsecondary vocational education by federal policy, changing demographics, and transformations in the ways firms and labor markets operate have had an impact on the growth of occupational-technical education in community colleges.

The U.S. General Accounting Office (1993) estimated that in the 1990–91 academic year, 93 percent of all two-year colleges offered an average of twenty-seven vocational programs. Nationwide, approximately 43 percent of the students in these colleges were enrolled in these programs. Results from the National Assessment of Vocational Education (Boesel, Rahn, and Diech, 1994) show a more positive picture of vocational education at the postsecondary than at the secondary level. Taking a critical view of vocational education overall, the authors commend aspects of postsecondary vocational education, saying, "Postsecondary vocational programs provide more structure than their secondary counterparts for students working toward a degree. . . . The economic outcomes for postsecondary vocational students are better than for secondary students. Postsecondary completers are more likely to find jobs related to their training, and even some coursetaking without completing a program seems to confer labor-market benefits. These advantages of postsecondary vocational education seem to be most pronounced in public community colleges" (pp. 17–18).

Research conducted by Grubb (1995) confirms this finding. In a secondary analysis of the Survey of Income and Program Participation, Grubb found that "both certificates and associate degrees increase the earnings of those who receive them—not, of course, by as much as a baccalaureate degree, which requires between two and four times as many credits, but, still, by substantial and statistically significant amounts" (p. iv). These findings are particularly evident for persons who complete a program and gain a credential, are considered nontraditional because of their gender or age, and/or who enter job-related training upon graduation.

Beyond the emphasis on occupationally oriented programs for their own students, increasingly community colleges are partnering with secondary schools to implement school-to-work-related educational reforms beginning at the high school level. Initiatives such as tech-prep and youth apprenticeship programs require community colleges to help high school youths make the transition to postsecondary education, where they can acquire more advanced academic and technical competencies needed for entry into the labor market. Although the involvement of community colleges has not yet fully developed with these school-to-work reforms (Bragg, Layton, and Hammons, 1994; Kazis, 1994; Boesel, Rahn, and Diech, 1994; Silverberg and Hershey, 1994), public policy encourages (and in the case of tech-prep legislation, mandates) two-year colleges to play a pivotal role.

Assessing Work-Based Learning in the Community College

For many years, students in community colleges have acquired work-related learning experiences while pursuing postsecondary education; however, these learning experiences are often not documented or monitored. Consequently, a wide array of approaches to work-based learning are used by community colleges, but no one standard definition or model exists. In a study dedicated to examining this issue of work-based learning at the two-year college, Bragg, Hamm, and Trinkle (1995) created a general definition, suggesting work-based learning programs are "instructional programs that *deliberately* use the workplace as a site for student learning" (p. 16). Work-based learning is further defined as "formal, structured, and strategically organized by instructional staff, employers, and sometimes other groups to link learning in the workplace to students' college-based learning experiences [and] to their career goals" (p. 16). Examples of work-based learning models identified in the study were professional-clinical training, cooperative education (co-op programs), formal registered apprenticeships, school-sponsored enterprises, and youth apprenticeships.

For community college students engaged in occupational-technical programs, work-based learning is fairly commonplace. Over three-quarters of community colleges engage students in work-based learning, and occupational-technical education and customized or contract training are two areas where students participate most readily in work-based learning opportunities (Bragg, Hamm, and Trinkle, 1995). On average, about 18 percent of community college students in occupational-technical education participate in some form of work-based learning. These findings corroborate results of the National Assessment of Vocational Education (NAVE), showing that work-based learning is fairly widespread at the two-year postsecondary level in occupational-technical education. In the NAVE study, Boesel, Rahn, and Diech (1994) found that "the range of work experience programs and the variety of linkages with employers and other non-university organizations is quite broad" (p. 143).

Of the numerous approaches to work-based learning, professional-clinical training and co-op programs are the most prevalent in community colleges (Bragg, Hamm, and Trinkle, 1995; Office of Technology Assessment, 1995;

Stern and others, 1994). Most community colleges offer health occupations programs, and nearly all of these programs require that students participate in the professional-clinical training. The Office of Technology Assessment (1995) reports that "the clinical training model has become the norm for preparation in all the medical occupations—ranging from nurse's aide through medical technologist to brain surgeon. . . . About 50 to 60 percent of all two-year colleges have at least one program that uses this model, and virtually all the programs are in the medical fields" (p. 65).

With the clinical training approach, students complete a combination of vocational and academic course work in classrooms and laboratories on campus. In addition, they engage in learning at the work site (clinic, hospital, nursing home) to obtain a credential in the profession. Although the practice is not nearly as widespread elsewhere as it is in the health occupations, professional fields such as education and law do engage community college students in clinical training. Disadvantages of this highly intensive work-based learning model are that students do not typically receive pay from employers for their time in clinical work experiences. Furthermore, programs utilizing the professional-clinical model are often the most expensive of any educational programs offered by community colleges.

Besides the clinical training model, the co-op is the most prevalent work-based learning model in the community college environment. The co-op has some important differences from the clinical training model because it is not as highly regulated by external bodies, nor is it as highly structured. It has the added benefit that students are usually paid for their time in the work setting. Like the professional-clinical model, however, co-op programs encourage a combination of vocational and academic course work that is coordinated with work experience, and students earn college credit for these experiences. Successful co-op programs usually require written agreements between schools and employers, work site training plans, and frequent supervision and ongoing assessment by a work-site and school coordinator (Stern and others, 1994). Two approaches are predominant in the co-op model: students are taught on campus for part of the day and work for part of the day, or students rotate between college and work on a semester-by-semester basis (Office of Technology Assessment, 1995). Although this second approach is more prevalent in four-year colleges and universities, it does occur in community colleges. The co-op is the work-based learning model of choice for fields such as business and marketing, engineering, agriculture, and human services.

Other forms of work-based learning are registered adult apprenticeships, school-sponsored enterprises, or youth apprenticeships, but these are utilized much less frequently by community colleges (Bragg, Hamm, and Trinkle, 1995). Casner-Lotto (1988) and Stern and others (1995) make similar observations about the preponderance of co-op programs and the very limited use of other work-based learning models. They report that, like co-op programs, registered apprenticeship programs are firmly planted in many two-year colleges, although little is known about the quality of these programs. It is evident, however, that most registered apprenticeship programs (at the postsecondary level) are in the skilled trades occupations, and most of the programs are very small. Further, Casner-Lotto (1988) reports that often the partnerships between education and labor on behalf of these programs are tenuous.

Little information exists about newer school-to-work models such as youth apprenticeship, particularly in relation to the postsecondary level. Corson and Silverberg (1993) describe evaluation results for fifteen school-to-work transition, youth apprenticeship demonstration programs funded by the U.S. Department of Labor. Their report documents that "none of the sites had any experience in implementing the postsecondary components of the program" (p. xi). Although not yet evident in practice, secondary-to-postsecondary articulation has been viewed as an essential part of youth apprenticeship programs. In this regard, when a work-based learning component is added, Kazis and Roche (1991) view youth apprenticeship programs as a logical extension of the tech-prep model (that is, integrated academic and vocational-technical curriculum delivered through two years of high school articulated with two years of college). Bragg, Hamm, and Trinkle (1995), however, found few community colleges utilize tech-prep or formal articulation agreements with secondary schools to create a progression of work-based learning from the secondary to postsecondary level. This finding is corroborated by results of a prior study by Bragg, Layton, and Hammons (1994) on tech-prep implementation, where only a minority of local tech-prep consortia in the United States were incorporating progressive and sequential work-based learning into curriculum reform at the secondary and postsecondary levels.

In addition, many community colleges have extensive experience in partnering with private sector firms to deliver related programs and services, such as customized or contract training, entrepreneurial training and small business development, and technology transfer (Bragg and Jacobs, 1991, 1993). Education-business partnerships can provide the basis for a diverse array of programs focused on workforce preparation, retraining, and upgrading (Grubb, Badway, Bell, and Kraskouskas, 1996). Some of these partnerships have contributed to work-based learning programs associated with the school-to-work transition as well (Bragg, Hamm, and Trinkle, 1995; Bragg and Hamm, 1996).

Connecting Activities in the Community College

Of the three components central to the STWOA (school-based learning, work-based learning, and connecting activities), connecting activities are the least understood. Although some employers participate in connecting activities, community colleges have primary responsibility for ensuring effective connections between school-based and work-based learning (Bragg, Hamm, and Trinkle, 1995). On the whole, an imbalance exists between education and employers in terms of who has responsibility for school-to-work tasks, with the contributions of community colleges far outweighing those of businesses.

Typically, community colleges have primary responsibility for performing all facets of connecting activities, including selecting and training workplace mentors; assessing and certifying students' academic, technical, and workplace skills; and placing students in full-time employment following graduation. Consequently, for more students to engage in school-to-work experiences, a greater sharing of responsibility must occur among colleges, employers, labor unions, and government agencies. If this sharing does not happen, community colleges are likely to develop school-to-work systems that require fewer resources, or they will abandon the concept altogether.

Implications for the Future

Few formal assessments have been conducted regarding the role of community college in school-to-work systems in the United States. Historically, two-year colleges have engaged in various school-to-work-oriented approaches, such as professional-clinical training, co-op programs, and traditional adult apprenticeships. School-sponsored enterprises, youth apprenticeships, and tech-prep programs are also evident in community colleges, although far less is known about these newer school-to-work models. Regardless of the model, community colleges take on the lion's share of responsibility for school-to-work programs in comparison to employers. Beyond supervising students engaged in work-based learning, many employers make minimal direct contributions to the school-to-work system.

Without doubt, the federal STWOA and similar state legislation (Smith, 1994) demonstrates heightened public interest in improving school-to-work systems. Although early activities associated with STWOA concentrated on high school youths, recent research shows community colleges make important contributions to school-to-work systems. Professional-clinical training and co-op programs are particularly prominent forms of work-based learning at the postsecondary level, and the benefits of these models are well documented. Of the newer approaches, tech-prep is most visible, although student outcomes data on it are extremely limited. Youth apprenticeships are even less evident at the postsecondary level.

As the nation continues efforts to implement school-to-work systems, it is increasingly important to document and disseminate the lessons learned by all of the organizations involved, including community colleges. With their strong tradition of forming education-business partnerships, community colleges appear strategically positioned to lead efforts to build school-to-work systems. Yet, the STWOA is heavily weighted toward secondary education, to ensure that high school students are better prepared to make the transition to either work or college. Educational pathways to assist students to move successfully between the secondary and postsecondary levels are valued, but they are not mandated. As such, reengineering to systematically link school-based and work-based learning at the secondary and postsecondary levels is rare. Consequently, more attention needs to be paid to creating educational pathways that do just that. With sufficient time and careful nurturing, eventually school-to-work systems may become routine in America's schools, colleges, and places of employment. If that goal is reached, it seems certain that community colleges will have played a prominent role.

References

Boesel, D., Rahn, M., and Diech, S. *National Assessment of Vocational Education: Final Report to Congress.* Washington, D.C.: U.S. Department of Education, Office of Educational Research and Improvement, July 1994.

Bragg, D., and Hamm, R. *Linking Colleges and Work: Exemplary Policies and Practices of Two-Year College Work-Based Learning Programs.* Berkeley: National Center for Research in Vocational Education, University of California, Berkeley, Apr. 1996.

Bragg, D., Hamm, R., and Trinkle, K. *Work-Based Learning in Two-Year Colleges in the United States.* Berkeley: National Center for Research in Vocational Education, University of California, Berkeley, Feb. 1995.

Bragg, D., and Jacobs, J. *A Conceptual Framework for Evaluating Community College Customized Training.* Berkeley: National Center for Research in Vocational Education, University of California, Berkeley, Nov. 1991.

Bragg, D., and Jacobs, J. "Establishing an Operational Definition of Customized Training. *Community College Review,* 1993, *21*(1), 15–24.

Bragg, D., Layton, J., and Hammons, F. *Tech Prep Implementation in the United States: Promising Trends and Lingering Challenges.* Berkeley: National Center for Research in Vocational Education, University of California, Berkeley, Sept. 1994.

Carnevale, A., Gainer, L., and Meltzer, A. *Workplace Basics: The Essential Skills Employers Want.* San Francisco: Jossey-Bass, 1990.

Casner-Lotto, J. *Successful Training Strategies: Twenty-Six Innovative Corporate Models.* San Francisco: Jossey-Bass, 1988.

Cohen, A., and Brawer, F. *The American Community College.* San Francisco: Jossey-Bass, 1989.

Corson, W., and Silverberg, M. *The School-to-Work/Youth Apprenticeship Demonstration Preliminary Findings.* Princeton, N.J.: Mathematica Policy Research, Oct. 1993.

Gray, K., and Herr, E. *Other Ways to Win.* Thousand Oaks, Calif.: Corwin Press, 1995.

Grubb, W. N. *The Returns to Education and Training in the Sub-baccalaureate Labor Market: Evidence from the Survey of Income and Program Participation 1984–1990.* Berkeley: National Center for Research in Vocational Education, University of California, Berkeley, May 1995.

Grubb, W. N., Badway, N., Bell, D., and Kraskouskas, E. *Community College Innovations in Workforce Preparation: Curriculum Integration and Tech-Prep.* Mission Viejo, Calif.: League for Innovation in the Community College, 1996.

Hamilton, S. F. *Apprenticeship for Adulthood: Preparing Youth for the Future.* New York: Free Press, 1990.

Kazis, R. "The Future Role of Two-Year Colleges in Improving the School-to-Work Transition." In L. Falcone and R. Mundhenk (eds.), *The Tech-Prep Associate Degree Challenge.* Washington, D.C.: American Association of Community Colleges, 1994.

Kazis, R., and Roche, B. "New U.S. Initiatives for the Transition from School to Work." Occasional paper no. 8. Geneva, Switzerland: International Labour Office, 1991.

Marshall, R., and Tucker, M. *Thinking for a Living: Education and the Wealth of Nations.* New York: Basic Books, 1992.

Nothdurft, W. E. *Schoolworks: Reinventing Public Schools to Create the Workforce of the Future.* Washington, D.C.: Brookings Institution, 1989.

Office of Technology Assessment. *Learning to Work: Making the Transition from School to Work* (OTA-EHR-637). Washington, D.C.: U.S. Government Printing Office, Sept. 1995.

Pennington, H. "The Evolution of the School-to-Work Opportunities Act." In J. F. Jennings (ed.), *National Issues in Education: Goals 2000 and School-to-Work*. Bloomington, Ind.: Phi Delta Kappa International, 1995.

Reich, R. B. *The Work of Nations. Preparing Ourselves for Twenty-First Century Capitalism.* New York: Vantage Books, 1991.

Reich, R. B. "Building a Framework for a School-to-Work Opportunities System." In J. F. Jennings (ed.), *National Issues in Education: Goals 2000 and School-to-Work*. Bloomington, Ind.: Phi Delta Kappa International, 1995.

Secretary's Commission on Achieving Necessary Skills. *What Work Requires of Schools: A SCANS Report for America 2000*. Washington, D.C.: U.S. Department of Labor, 1991.

Silverberg, M., and Hershey, A. *The Emergence of Tech Prep at the State and Local Levels.* Washington, D.C.: U.S. Department of Education, Sept. 1994.

Smith, C. L. *A Review of Youth Apprenticeship Legislation at the State Level.* Paper presented at the American Educational Research Association meeting, New Orleans, Apr. 1994.

Stern, D., Finkelstein, N., Stone, J., Lattig, J., and Dornsife, C. *School to Work: Research on Programs in the United States.* Bristol, Pa.: Falmer Press, 1994.

U.S. General Accounting Office. *Transition from School to Work: Linking Education and Work-site Training* (HRD-91–105). Washington, D.C.: U.S. Government Printing Office, Aug. 1993.

DEBRA D. BRAGG is associate professor in the College of Education at the University of Illinois, Urbana-Champaign.

MILDRED BARNES GRIGGS is dean of the College of Education at the University of Illinois, Urbana-Champaign.

*This chapter examines the ways in which benchmarking, a continuous
quality improvement process, can be used to define the quality of
school-to-work systems for community college practitioners.*

Benchmarking for Quality Curriculum:
The Heart of School-to-Work

Margaret A. Ellibee, Sarah A. Mason

A high-quality curriculum is an integral part of any school-to-work (STW) initiative, at any educational level. The STW curriculum can be thought of as the
engine that drives the design and development of the STW system, within and
across institutions and programs. At its best, the STW curriculum presents
activities that transfer learning and knowledge to real-world situations, integrating career and workplace experiences that are rich in, and applicable to,
diverse contexts. By viewing their STW curriculum through this particular
lens, postsecondary educators can envision vocational and academic content
that will integrate learner experiences, active and applied instructional practices, and student-focused assessment. However, incorporating these visions
into new and existing curricula poses a variety of challenges to community and
technical college personnel.

Recently, a host of factors has influenced curriculum development and quality, including the advent of national skill standards and a growing emphasis on
integrated and sequenced courses that link school- and work-based learning.
Community and technical colleges, seeking to respond to these new educational
challenges, have adopted a variety of approaches to reforming curriculum design.
In fact, the National Center for Research in Vocational Education (NCRVE) has
identified eight different models community and technical colleges have used to
design and integrate occupational and academic education:

1. Integrating general education requirements
2. Developing applied academic courses
3. Incorporating academic skills into occupational programs
4. Infusing academic models into expanded occupational courses

5. Developing multidisciplinary courses that combine academic perspectives and occupational concerns
6. Designing tandem cluster courses in various learning communities
7. Developing colleges within colleges
8. Generating alternative occupational programming (Grubb and Kraskouskas, 1992)

As a result of these new challenges, educators are often left with "what," "how," and "why" questions about the development and quality of their curriculum: "What should be in my school-to-work curriculum?" "How will I know if my curriculum is any good?" "Why should I review my curriculum now, when all these changes are taking place?" In our dynamic educational climate, these questions are particularly relevant. Educators seeking answers need a framework to uncover emerging practices that focus efforts in quality STW curriculum design.

This chapter examines how benchmarking, a continuous quality improvement process, can be used to define and improve the quality of STW curricula. Adapted from business and industry, the benchmarking process begins with a self-study. The self-study includes a systematic review of established goals and objectives, followed by a self-assessment of existing practices and collection of supporting information and data. The next step in the benchmarking process involves team members learning about emerging "best practices" and how they can be adapted or adopted to improve local initiatives. Conducted collaboratively by a broad range of practitioners, the benchmarking process generates a shared, in-depth understanding of local practices through identification of specific objectives, critical reflection, a focus on strengths and weaknesses, and the adoption or adaptation of "best practices" (Camp, 1989; Spendolini, 1992; Tucker, 1996). Through benchmarking, practitioners can effectively review and improve curriculum design. The process incorporates the goals of national educational initiatives (such as Goals 2000 and the School-to-Work Opportunities Act) as well as state and local strategic and school improvement plans. In addition, benchmarking uses valid criteria and standards of quality. The benchmarking process provides a structure for review teams to conduct a self-assessment of current curriculum components. These components reflect unique aspects of academic and occupational disciplines, while providing a common foundation to review the quality of content and pedagogy. The component-based structure of the benchmarking process enables the community or technical college to review a variety of curricula and adapt particular quality components to meet specific needs.

The National Consortium of Product Quality (NCPQ) standards and indicators, developed through the NCRVE, offer educators a set of quality criteria to guide curriculum review. Designed to assess STW curriculum, the NCPQ standards and indicators represent qualitative ideals and supporting attributes of high-quality STW curriculum. Working in concert, the standards and indicators can guide the review team in benchmarking the degree of quality in their STW curriculum content, instruction, student assessment, and equity and diversity.

Internally, once the review team has documented the existing curriculum, they can compare their practices and products with others' to identify "best practices." To complete the cycle, these "best practices" are then incorporated into the larger planning process, ensuring continuous curriculum improvement. As a result, the curriculum review team integrates relevant information (specific skills, diversity considerations, performance levels) and existing benchmarks of quality (Bonnet, 1981) and is better equipped to soundly assess STW curricula and related course materials.

A Step-by-Step Benchmarking Process

The remainder of this chapter details a step-by-step benchmarking process for review teams to guide their evaluation of STW curricula.

Step 1: Create a Benchmarking Team for Curriculum Review. STW systems represent systemic reform initiatives that encourage a broad collaboration of partners to develop new approaches to education. This type of reform challenges educators to expand their vision to serve the mutual needs of students, K–12 schools, community and technical colleges, business, and the community. In this context, creating a quality STW curriculum entails integration both *within* occupational and academic areas and *across* educational and business-oriented organizations. Creating mutually inclusive teams is therefore essential to a quality curriculum review process. Curriculum review teams that involve representatives from all groups ensure that each has the opportunity to express their organizational needs. Moreover, a team including a diverse set of representatives incorporates a broad range of expertise and promotes creativity and ownership in the review process.

The continuous improvement process of benchmarking requires such a collaborative review team. When conducted collaboratively by a broad range of local practitioners, the benchmarking process generates a shared, in-depth understanding of curriculum products and practices by identifying specific objectives, reflecting on actual products and practices, and identifying strengths and weaknesses. Ultimately, benchmarking aims to focus discussion on the specific areas needing improvement.

Step 2: Identify What to Benchmark. Teams embarking on the benchmarking process should first review existing strategic plans at the institution or program level and related missions, goals, and objectives. Information obtained from these documents will help guide team members as they select the appropriate curriculum for review.

In selecting the curriculum to review, several other considerations should be involved in the decision-making process. First, teams may choose to review a variety of curricula that incorporate integration activities, or they may focus on a single curricular aspect.

Second, the intentions of the teaching-learning goals for any educational program must be taken into account when selecting the curriculum for review. For example, teams may choose to review an existing "high-quality" STW curriculum that includes student learning objectives (for example, what a student should know and be able to do), effective instructional practice, and student-focused authentic assessment. The components presented below provide teams with a snapshot of quality standards:

Content: High-quality STW content focuses on the integration of academic foundations into career development, life skills, and occupational competencies.

Instruction: Instruction should include the development of problem solving, communication, and reasoning skills of all students through authentic experiences within the classroom and community environments.

Assessment: Assessments in high-quality STW curricula are student-focused in the measurement of attitudes, knowledge, and skills as well as in their application to problem solving within the classroom and workplace environment.

Equity and Diversity: High-quality STW curricula reflect the values of equity and diversity.

Step 3: Complete Self-Assessment. The NCPQ standards and indicators, presented in Exhibit 2.1, form the foundation of the self-assessment step in this benchmarking process. The self-assessment process begins with team members discussing what is currently in place. Team members examine the curriculum by answering the indicator questions in relation to their existing curriculum or to a specific curriculum product. They are encouraged to provide a rationale supporting their conclusions for each indicator. Relevant data should also be presented to provide a baseline to use when comparing curricula, identifying "best practices," and measuring performance improvement. Data may be obtained from such sources as pre-and post-assessment results, instructor journal entries, student interest inventories, or field-test data.

Next, team members identify areas of strength and areas that need improvement. Areas of strength are those that currently meet or exceed the NCPQ standards. Those areas needing improvement are those that do not fully support the standards; these are the areas that should be targeted for improvement.

Step 4: Identify Best Practices for Comparison and Learning. Once team members have assessed and prioritized areas to improve, their next step should be to seek out others who have successfully dealt with such curriculum issues. These "best practices" then become a source of ideas, information, and strategies for adapting and improving local curriculum. Examples of "best practice" curricula may be found in a variety of ways: networking with colleagues from other institutions, searching professionally developed curriculum guides, searching curriculum sites on the Internet, reviewing ERIC resources, and contacting the NCPQ through the NCRVE.

Exhibit 2.1. The NCPQ Standards and Indicators

Content Standards and Indicators

STW curricula must focus on the integration of academic foundations into career development, life skills, and occupational competencies.

To what extent has the content incorporated validated skills, tasks, and competencies to consistently and continually reinforce concepts?

To what extent do the skills and competencies presented in the product correspond to competencies and skills indicated in the SCANS report?

To what extent does the product include documentation (for example, a matrix) of validated occupational, academic, career, and life skills and competencies to show where and how those skills and competencies are being incorporated?

To what extent does the product identify performance levels for skills and competencies?

To what extent is the content current?

To what extent is the content accurate?

To what extent is the content sequenced from basic to more complex concepts or coherent clusters?

To what extent are the content objectives and learner objectives aligned?

To what extent is the content presented in an interesting and appealing manner geared toward diverse student audiences?

To what extent are career development, career awareness and mobility, and citizenship incorporated into the instructional content?

Are vocational and academic skills integrated?

Are employability and life skills (for example, getting to work on time) included?

Is inclusive language used?

Are diversity and commonalities among people recognized?

Are contributions from people of diverse backgrounds recognized?

Is transferability of learned skills and knowledge emphasized?

Instructional Standards and Indicators

STW curricula, through active and applied learning experiences in school, community, and work-based settings, must enable students to acquire problem-solving, communication, and reasoning strategies.

To what extent do the instructional strategies include active and meaningful learning experiences that correspond to stated student outcomes?

To what extent do the instructional strategies include teaching techniques that enhance the SCANS thinking skills: creative thinking, decision making, problem solving, seeing things in the mind's eye, knowing how to learn, and reasoning?

To what extent can the suggested instructional strategies be adapted to different learning styles?

To what extent do the instructional strategies (that is, activities and projects) reflect the diversity of today's workforce?

To what extent do the instructional strategies incorporate team or small group projects?

To what extent do the instructional strategies encourage students to interact with each other, instructors, and the community?

To what extent do the instructional strategies develop students' critical thinking and problem-solving skills?

To what extent do the instructional strategies develop students' skills in writing, speaking, listening, and following directions?

To what extent do the instructional strategies provide the students with real-world experiences (both in and out of the classroom) that reinforce academic and technology applications?

Exhibit 2.1. *(continued)*

Student Assessment Standards and Indicators

Assessments within STW programs must be student-focused in measuring attitudes, knowledge, and skills and they must measure problem-solving skills within both the classroom and the workplace environment.

To what extent are student teams, as well as the individual student, assessed?
To what extent does the assessment tool measure the attitude, knowledge, or skill presented in the material?
To what extent does the assessment process include feedback and alternative testing opportunities?
To what extent are performance and portfolio assessments used to measure student knowledge and skills?
To what extent can the assessments detect change over time?
To what extent are appropriate assessment methods provided that directly reflect student outcomes?

Equity and Diversity Standards and Indicators

STW curricula must reflect content that portrays and celebrates the active participation of all individuals in the nation's workforce, communities, and educational institutions.

To what extent is the material balanced to reflect the experiences, contributions, voices, and perspectives of all groups?
To what extent does the content challenge traditional cultural assumptions?

The NCPQ provides research-based evaluation and technical assistance for local, state, and national developers of curricula and instructional materials. The consortium assists in curriculum networking, identifies curriculum search sources, and reviews submitted curriculum or printed instructional material.

Step 5: Create an Action Plan for Curriculum Improvement. Team members should summarize information detailing strategies, sources, and the pros and cons of implementing changes in their curriculum. Teams must then reconvene to review the information and develop "improvement action plans," thus linking the information gathered through the benchmarking process to the curriculum planning process.

Step 6: Revisit the Curriculum. As these strategies are adopted, the level of curriculum implementation should be continuously monitored. Review teams need to pay particular attention to determining whether the adopted changes have effectively contributed to student learning. With an eye toward the future, this activity also helps the review team develop new insight and directions for future curriculum design.

Meaningful Curriculum Benchmarking: Where Can It Lead?

Completing the benchmarking process will reward community and technical colleges with a better understanding of their existing STW curriculum and with new directions for student-centered teaching and learning. Using this process to assess STW curricula will require teams to become intimately involved in assessing curriculum components. An integral knowledge of the quality status of STW curriculum components will not only benefit student learners but will also engage team members as learners in the benchmarking curriculum review process.

References

Bonnet, D. "Five Phases of Purposeful Inquiry." In R. S. Brandt (ed.), *Applied Strategies for Curriculum Evaluation.* Alexandria, Va.: Association for Supervision and Curriculum Development, 1981.

Camp, R. *Benchmarking: The Search for Industry Best Practices That Lead to Superior Performance.* White Plains, N.Y.: Quality Resources, 1989.

Grubb, W. N., and Kraskouskas, E. "A Time to Every Purpose: Integrating Occupational and Academic Education in Community Colleges and Technical Institutes." *NCRVE Change Agent,* 1992 (No. MDS-251), pp. 6–7.

Spendolini, M. *The Benchmarking Book.* New York: American Management Association, 1992.

Tucker, S. *Benchmarking: A Guide for Educators.* Thousand Oaks, Calif.: Corwin Press, 1996.

MARGARET A. ELLIBEE is codirector of the National Consortium for Product Quality and outreach specialist for the Center on Education and Work, University of Wisconsin, Madison.

SARAH A. MASON is outreach specialist for the Center on Education and Work, University of Wisconsin, Madison.

Partnerships between educators and local businesses are essential,
required components of school-to-work initiatives. Building these
partnerships does not need to be complicated if you just follow
a few simple steps.

Building Partnerships

Mary J. Kisner, Maralyn J. Mazza, David R. Liggett

Partnerships between all levels of education and local business and industry are essential components of today's school reform initiatives. However, while the definition of the partnership has not changed much over the last twenty-five years, the role of the partnership in effective school reform has shifted dramatically. A successful partnership today will often include an entire community of educational institutions and local businesses collaborating to improve the educational experiences of all its students. This chapter will address the definition of a partnership, the shift of focus over the last few decades concerning the role of the partnership in educational reform, and steps to implementing partnerships that are strategically beneficial to all.

Defining a Partnership

A partnership is a continued cooperative effort or agreement to collaborate to generate ideas or to pool resources for a mutually acceptable set of purposes. This effort may attack a specific problem or support an ongoing project of wider scope (Forrest, 1992; Hemmings, 1984; Shive and Rogus, 1979). Partnerships for school-to-work activities have many of the characteristics of a strategic alliance in business, where collaborations between firms and other organizations are developed for important strategic reasons (Walters, Peters, and Dess, 1994).

Changing Focus of Partnerships

The focus of partnerships to support education—especially the roles of secondary schools, postsecondary schools, and business and industry—has changed during this century. During the first half of this century, business was often involved in public school planning and decision making. Education and business agreed on the main purpose of public schools—to prepare young people for work. However, in the mid 1960s to late 1970s it became less acceptable to have business input, as organized parent and community groups became more active. Businesses soon lost touch with what was happening in public education on a day-to-day basis (Timpane, 1984).

By the late 1970s and early 1980s there was an atmosphere of mistrust between school and business. Business issued "expectations" for schools (stricter rules of discipline), while educators feared business support of any kind might grow into "inappropriate influence." Many educators suggested that limits be placed on business involvement in the schools (Cramer, 1982; Lesher, 1977; Ozmon, 1982).

During the early 1980s business involvement was defined and limited to an advisory role, thus the growth of "advisory committees." These committees of individuals outside the education profession were selected to advise on a program or aspect of a program (Cochran, Phelps, and Cochran, 1980; Kline, 1983). Permitted involvement might include mock interviews for students, money for equipment, managerial expertise and new technologies, scholarships, and classroom materials (Crawford-Clark, 1985; Hansen and Schergens, 1982; Jensen, 1983; Ozmon, 1982; Shinn, 1985). It seemed to be understood that business had no compelling need to support schools, except by paying taxes, and schools could gain money for projects now and political allies later. Most business activities in schools were brief and episodic (Mann, 1984). School-business partnerships were not seen as a way to dramatically improve educational attainment nationwide (Woodside, 1984). Postsecondary schools and community colleges, positioned between the secondary school and the world of work, often had an undefined role. They were contracted to provide training programs for workers, often tailoring programs to the needs of business and industry (Gold and Charner, 1993) but often were not involved in secondary school activities.

Between 1983 and 1988, the number of education-business partnerships more than tripled. As they expanded in number, they also changed in character, from single-purpose projects to much more complex, multiactor collaborative agreements (Lankard, 1995). The nature of education-business partnerships has evolved in the last ten years from an advisory relationship to a collaborative, reform-driven effort, with whole communities involved ("Quid Pro Quo," 1994). The tech-prep movement required that responsibility for the educational system be shared by educators, employers, workers, parents, students, and others. Each group has a vested interest in the evolution of tech-prep programs (Bragg, 1995). The school-to-work movement also makes business–postsecondary school partners essential components in the education process for all students (Gray and Herr, 1995). However, both education and business are working to build successful partnerships to benefit all players.

Steps to Building Partnerships

The steps to building an effective partnership for school-to-work activities include reviewing your mission, selecting strategic partners, setting clearly defined goals, maintaining the relationship, and evaluating the partnership for success. Before establishing a partnership, all partners must internally review their basic mission. This review provides the foundation for developing relationships with strategic partners that will enhance their missions.

Selecting Strategic Partners

Strategic partners for school-to-work activities are not partners of convenience. Partners must be chosen for the strengths they bring to the relationship. The goal is to develop synergism between the contributions of the partners, resulting in a win-win situation for both or all of them (Walters, Peters, and Dess, 1994). Each partner must first know its own strengths, needs, and resources. Developing trust is central to the success of the alliance, because partners must be willing to share important, strategic information. Secondary schools may need to share data about dropout rates, graduation rates, and assessment scores. Postsecondary schools may need to share their completion and placement rates. Businesses may need to share information about their training needs, their pay scales, and the quality of their products.

Strategically, partners for a school-to-work initiative should be chosen to enhance specific components of the system. For example, to enhance school-based activities, partners might be chosen because they provide career awareness for all students, in all aspects of an industry. A partnership with a hospital, for example, could provide opportunities for middle school students to interview workers in all areas of the health care industry to discover the academic skills required to succeed in the health care field. A postsecondary institution with health certification programs could enhance these opportunities with presentations by graduates to the secondary students.

The hospital could provide the work-based component and include placements for internships for secondary and postsecondary students in health occupations clusters. To be successful, these placements should correlate directly with students' career goals and be supervised by a workplace mentor. The connecting activities partners might involve a postsecondary school serving as a connecting link to help students find appropriate placements for job-shadowing experiences. Selecting the appropriate strategic partners for the first project is the first step in building an effective partnership. The next step is to set realistic goals.

Goal Setting

Partners begin their planning by setting goals. Clearly defined goals help all partners strive toward the same objective, in the same time frame. To begin a partnership, a small project or goal should be chosen to phase in the relationship. This will increase the potential for success by allowing trust to grow between alliance partners. Working together on small projects initially helps develop this trust (Slowinski, 1992). "Each partner has a chance to gauge the skills and contributions of the other, and further investment can then be considered" (Walters, Peters, and Dess, 1994, p. 8).

Winning together on a project of any scale is a great way to build trust and overcome differences, and it usually serves as a precursor to more ambitious joint efforts. Partners must first determine their goals and review their resources, noting which resources the other could use and benefit from if the two were to work together. A manufacturing firm hoping to entice more students to consider careers in robotics technology might partner with a postsecondary program and a high school vocational program to offer field trips, speakers, job shadowing, internship, and cooperative work experiences for students. To begin the project, the firm might first establish just one type of experience with one classroom of students. After one such program had been successful, it could be expanded into other experiences. Phasing-in smaller projects should help partners determine if future ventures are viable, while keeping risks low.

Maintaining a Partnership

A formal partnership agreement is essential to the partnership's success. This agreement must identify the key players and their responsibilities, a time line for the project, milestones to document progress, and the desired outcomes of the project. This document need not be complicated (Stainback, Winborne, and Davis, 1983), but it must be built on discussions about how the project will be evaluated. This should be a partnership for mutual benefit, "not to subsidize each other or poach on each other's prerogatives" (Harbaugh, 1985, p. 27). The agreement should include a method of evaluation and an exit strategy, or a description of how the relationship will be ended if outcomes are not met. And when milestones *are* successfully met, don't forget to celebrate the success together—even publicize it. This enhances the possibility of future success. Through a process of ongoing review and assessment, single-project partnerships can evolve into multiactor partnerships for the benefit of all (Hull, 1995).

Conclusion

Education-business partnerships are essential to the success of school-to-work programs. Here are some questions to help you consider whether you are ready to begin forming such partnerships:

- Have you reviewed your mission?
- Have you selected strategic partners?

- Have you chosen a small project (or goal) with measurable outcomes and predefined milestones to phase-in the relationship? Have these outcomes and milestones been documented in writing?
- Have you identified each partner's key players and their responsibilities in writing?
- Have you created an evaluation method?
- Have you defined an exit strategy in case the partnership proves unsuccessful or objectives are not achieved?

A case in point: South Hills Business School is a private two-year school located in central Pennsylvania, with a student body of nearly four hundred students. The school is on the forefront of the school-to-work movement in the county, with a long history of matching its program offerings to employer needs. For the past year they have been reaching out to the local secondary schools to build tech-prep and school-to-work partnerships. As Maralyn Mazza, the school's director, explains, "We always had close relationships with local employers, but we found we had to take the initiative to build tech-prep partnerships with the local high schools. We started our partnerships with the superintendents and principals. After the school boards approved the relationship, we moved on to work cooperatively with the counselors and teachers. We shared the entry-level standards we required for our programs and encouraged high schools to modify their curriculum so students would have the needed competencies when they arrived at our school. We now have articulation agreements with twenty-four schools. These tech-prep partnerships have been successful in that we have better-prepared students entering our school and, subsequently, better-qualified job candidates leaving at graduation time. Our continuing placement rate of 85 to 90 percent can attest to the quality of our graduates."

The success of this program has built a level of trust between the high school and South Hills staff. South Hills now has several staff members whose time is devoted to outreach activities in the local schools. As South Hills plans to expand to other partnership activities in the county, Maralyn Mazza expects the agreements to become more formal documents. In the beginning, the most important thing was to build trust between partners. The partners can now build on this trust and develop more complex school-to-work activities.

References

Bragg, D. D. "Tech Prep: Where Are We Now?" *Vocational Education Journal,* 1995, 70(4), 18–23.

Cochran, L. H., Phelps, L. A., and Cochran, L. L. (1980). *Advisory Committees in Action.* Boston: Allyn & Bacon, 1980.

Cramer, J. "But Savvy School Leaders Raise the Issue of Education Ethics." *The American School Board Journal,* 1982, 169(3), 36–38.

Crawford-Clark, B. "When Schools and Businesses Pair Off, Both Can Live Happily Ever After." *The American School Board Journal,* 1985, 172(2), 36–37, 40.

Forrest, J. E. "Management Aspects of Strategic Partnering." *Journal of General Management,* 1992, *17*(4), 25–40.

Gold, G. G., and Charner, I. "Employer-Paid Tuition Aid: Hidden Treasure." *Educational Record,* 1993, *64*(2), 45–47.

Gray, K. C., and Herr, E. L. *Other Ways to Win: Creating Alternatives for High School Graduates.* Thousand Oaks, Calif.: Corwin Press, 1995.

Hansen, S., and Schergens, B. "Business/Education Partnerships: Making Them Education's Business." *Phi Delta Kappan,* 1982, *63*(10), 94–95.

Harbaugh, M. "Schools Are Bullish on Business." *Instructor,* May 1985, pp. 24–27.

Hemmings, M. B. *New Steps in Public-Private Partnerships.* Columbus, Ohio: National Center for Research in Vocational Education, 1984. (ED 253 702)

Hull, D. *The Revolution That's Changing Education: Who Are You Calling Stupid?* Waco, Tex.: Center for Occupational Research and Development, 1995.

Jensen, P. "Private Sector Initiatives in Education." *NAASP Bulletin,* Apr. 1983, pp. 17–19.

Kline, B. "Industry-Education Linkages." *Industrial Education,* 1983, *71*(8), 15.

Lankard, B. A. *Business/Education Partnerships* (Digest No. 156, EDO-CE-95-156). Columbus, Ohio: ERIC Clearinghouse on Adult, Career, and Vocational Education, 1995. (ED 383 856)

Lesher, R. L. *Education and Business: Partners for Human Progress. NAASP Bulletin,* 1977, *61*(413), 98–103.

Mann, D. "It's Up to You to Steer Those School/Business Partnerships." *The American School Board Journal,* 1984, *171*(10), 20–24.

Ozmon, H. "Adopt-A-School: Definitely Not Business As Usual." *Phi Delta Kappan,* 1982, *63*(5), 350–351.

"Quid Pro Quo." *Vocational Education Journal,* 1994, *69*(5), 22–23, 39.

Shinn, L. "Choosing Equipment? Involve Employers!" *Vocational Education Journal,* 1985, *60*(5), 30–32.

Shive, J., and Rogus, J. F. "The School-Business Partnership: A Concept Revitalized." *The Clearing House,* 1979, *52*(6), 286–290.

Slowinski, G. "The Human Touch in Successful Strategic Alliances." *Mergers & Acquisitions,* July-Aug. 1992, pp. 44–47.

Stainback, G. H., Winborne, C. R., and Davis, S. J. "Our School/Business Partnership Is a Smash." *The American School Board Journal,* 1983, *170*(9), 42.

Timpane, M. "Business Has Rediscovered the Public Schools." *Phi Delta Kappan,* 1984, *65*(6), 389–392.

Walters, B. A., Peters, S., and Dess, G. G. "Strategic Alliances and Joint Ventures: Making Them Work." *Business Horizons,* 1994, *37*(4), 5–10.

Woodside, W. S. "The Corporate Role in Public Education." *Social Policy,* 1984, *15*(2), 44–45.

MARY J. KISNER is assistant professor in the Workforce Education and Development program at Pennsylvania State University, University Park, Pennsylvania.

MARALYN J. MAZZA is director of South Hills Business School at State College, Pennsylvania.

DAVID R. LIGGETT is assistant director of the Centre County Technical School, Pleasant Gap, Pennsylvania.

The purpose of articulation is to create a partnership between high schools, colleges, and business and industry in order to promote a seamless transition for the student from one education experience to another.

The Art of Articulation: Connecting the Dots

David A. Just, Dewey A. Adams

The Carl D. Perkins Applied Technology and Vocational Education Act of 1990 began the establishment of tech-prep programs on a national scale. This legislation was the driving force responsible for a nationwide effort to develop tech-prep articulation agreements between secondary and postsecondary institutions ("2 + 2 programs"). These articulation agreements have provided a solid foundation for the implementation of school-to-work systems on a state-by-state basis.

New tech-prep articulation agreements will challenge the existing community college articulation process. These new agreements virtually guarantee students a seamless curriculum from high school through the associate degree, ensuring that students will no longer have to take duplicate courses.

Two-year colleges will not be able to "dust off" old articulation agreements and change the names of a few courses to become participants in tech-prep programs. Educational institutions should be pushing for systemic change (Total Quality Management) and move toward a customer-student focus during the tech-prep articulation process.

Many two-year institutions may be concerned that tech-prep programs could conflict with their student enrollment-retention program. If high school students are given advanced standing in enough courses, it would follow that their associate degree programs would be shortened, potentially reducing second-year student enrollment figures.

An innovative response to this dilemma is the creation of advanced skill certificates. Yes, students do have the option of graduating early from their associate degree programs. The advanced skill certificates developed for tech-prep students take them beyond the courses required for an associate degree. Many of these certificate programs can be developed to assist students during their transfer to four-year institutions. These certificates then give students an option to continue at their two-year college for advanced skill development.

Articulation

Articulation arrangements involve specific written agreements between high schools, vocational-technical schools, and postsecondary institutions to facilitate a smooth transition for students to associate degree programs and beyond. These agreements eliminate duplication of course content from one education experience to another. In many instances, they guarantee the student enrollment at the postsecondary institution. See, for example, Penn State's articulation policy at http://milkman.cac.psu.edu/~jpc2/tc.html.

There are many generic formats for developing articulation agreements, and many states have left this activity to the discretion of those educational institutions and agencies that have been charged with their development. Therefore, there is no one universal model utilized in the development of articulation agreements. The following are four articulation design variations that have emerged from research (Hammons and Maignan, 1995):

1. One general agreement that articulates all of the established programs of study.
2. One formal articulation agreement developed for each of the programs of study. If there are ten programs of study, there will be ten separate articulation agreements.
3. One formal articulation agreement for a varied number of programs of study within a common career path.
4. Multiple articulation agreements to support only one program of study. If ten high schools feed into a two-year college's program of study, there may be multiple articulation agreements for that one program of study.

The number of articulated credit hours a student can earn by participating in a tech-prep or school-to-work program of study varies from program to program and from state to state. A sample of a typical articulation agreement between a high school and a two-year college appears in Exhibit 4.1.

Collaborative Planning

The development of well-articulated and integrated curricula requires collaborative planning among school administrators, academic and occupational teachers, employers, and labor unions (U.S. Department of Education, 1996).

School administrators facilitate the development of integrated curricula by decentralizing management and adopting decision-making models that promote interaction among teachers across disciplines. Administrators can also

Exhibit 4.1. Sample Articulation Agreement

NORTH CENTRAL TECHNICAL COLLEGE
DIVISION OF CORPORATE SERVICES
AGREEMENT OF ARTICULATION
between
NORTH CENTRAL TECHNICAL COLLEGE
DIVISION OF CORPORATE SERVICES
and
MANSFIELD CITY SCHOOLS
WELDING TECHNOLOGY PROGRAM

This agreement is based on a review of the Welding program at Mansfield City Schools and the Welding Technology program at North Central Technical College. Joint faculty and administrative review and discussion of these programs establishes the following agreement:

Students completing and graduating from the two-year Welding program at Mansfield City Schools will receive credit for the courses listed below when the following criteria are met:

1. An application to NCTC must be submitted within two years of high school graduation.
2. Articulation credit must be requested in the NCTC Office of Student Records.
3. A high school transcript must be submitted to the NCTC Office of Student Records.
4. The student must have received a grade of "B" or better in the occupational program and an overall high school grade average of "C" or better.

WLD 105	Welding Cutting Principles and Basic Arc	5 credit hours
WLD 110	Advanced Shielded Metal Arc Welding	4 credit hours
WLD 115	Welding Symbols and Prints	2 credit hours
WLD 120	Gas Metal Arc Welding	4 credit hours
WLD 215	Welding Power Sources	3 credit hours
WLD 220	Gas Tungsten Arc Welding	3 credit hours
WLD 225	Introduction to Nondestructive Testing	4 credit hours
	Total	25 credit hours

In addition to the above articulation credit, students, with the recommendation of their vocational program instructor, may take the Credit-by-Examination test for the following courses.

DRD 115	Engineering Drawing	4 credit hours
MFG 121	Manufacturing Processes	4 credit hours
PHY 114	General Physics	4 credit hours
REF 120	Sheet Metal Fabrication	5 credit hours
WLD 205	Applied Metallurgy	4 credit hours
WLD 210	Structural Steel Fabrication	3 credit hours
WLD 230	Pipe Welding	5 credit hours
WLD 235	Advanced Materials Joining Systems	4 credit hours
WLD 240	Welding Codes and Procedures	3 credit hours

This agreement of articulation shall continue in effect until further review by either or both parties results in the need for a new agreement, or until discontinued by either or both parties.

Source: North Central Technical College (Mansfield, Ohio) Catalog, 1995–1996.

provide teachers with time for professional development as well as time to work together on curriculum issues (U.S. Department of Education, 1996).

Collaboration among teachers is essential. Teachers need the opportunity to work together as teams to develop alternative instructional strategies. A number of school systems (secondary and postsecondary) offer teachers time in the summer to work with employers and labor unions to develop curricula that integrate applied academics with work-based learning. These internships help teachers acquire experiences that help them apply industry-related skills and expectations to their classroom instruction.

Employers and labor unions play key roles in the development of integrated curricula. They enhance curriculum development by providing examples of how concepts learned in the classroom are applied in the workplace. Structured work-based learning enhances school-based instruction by giving students the opportunity to try out their newly acquired knowledge and skills in a real-world setting. The development of national skills standards by industry leaders gives employers and labor unions documented job profiles that help educators identify what particular industries expect their workers to know and to be able to perform (U.S. Department of Education, 1996).

Toward Systemic Change

The purpose of articulation is to create a partnership of excellence between high schools, colleges, and business and industry. Educational institutions should be pushing for systemic change in their systems and not simply relabeling current programs in high school to match current programs in higher education. For example, the state of Ohio is utilizing a new process to develop curricula via the technical competency profile (TCP), a method of identifying the occupational, academic, and employability competencies that must be developed during grades 11 and 12 and the two years of an associate degree program to prepare students for technician-level positions.

The TCP process ensures that the competencies are agreed upon by all participating members of the advisory group, which includes business and industry experts, labor representatives, high school teachers, and two-year college faculty members (see Figures 4.1 and 4.2). Once agreement is reached, a seamless curriculum from high school through the associate degree is developed.

The unique portion of this process occurs upon completion of the curriculum. At this time the high school teachers and two-year college faculty members meet to discuss how best to deliver the curriculum while building on local strengths. Each competency in the profile is matched according to the grade level at which it needs to be mastered. This ensures that students will no longer have to take duplicate courses. The faculty members may also decide on the best location to deliver particular courses. Colleges share laboratories, facilities, classrooms, and equipment with high schools. High school tech-prep students may be bused to the colleges to use state-of-the-art equipment, thereby avoiding duplicating expensive resources. These students receive high school–level occupational competencies at the colleges.

Figure 4.1. Technical Competency Profile Process

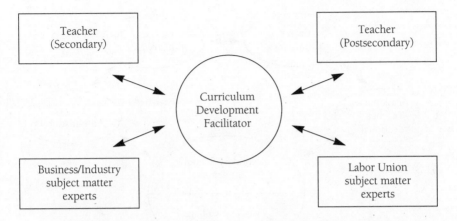

1. Analyze area labor market data.
2. Define exit occupations, first those at the end of the two-year degree or apprenticeship program and then the high school exit occupations that support those pursuits.
3. Convene consortium representatives from business, industry, and labor to identify competencies.
4. Convene consortium representatives from secondary and postsecondary education in the areas of communication, mathematics, and science for the purpose of examining technologies (identified by the exit occupations) and assigning performance levels to each competency at biannual points, and query the clarity of the competencies identified by business, industry, and labor.
5. Reconvene both groups to resolve questions regarding the competency list, determine the education and training needs of faculty, discuss delivery options for possible work-based or work-site components, identify material and equipment deficits within the consortium that would inhibit delivery, and voice concerns regarding marketing to students, parents, counselors, other teachers, and administrators.
6. Form committees to develop the actual projects, problems, lessons, modules, courses of study, and eventually curriculum guides for the various components—some interdisciplinary, some integrated, some discipline-specific—of the tech-prep program.
7. Produce a composite tech-prep curriculum pathway that alerts students, parents, and counselors to secondary and postsecondary course requirements.

Source: List adapted from ERIC Clearinghouse on Adult Career and Vocational Education, 1996.

Since 1993, fifty-six TCPs have been developed among the twenty-four tech-prep consortia throughout Ohio. The thirty-six two-year colleges involved with the twenty-four consortia have used these profiles in their tech-prep articulation process. The response from faculty members (secondary and postsecondary) involved in the TCP process has been positive, with many saying that TCP provides them with an opportunity to develop their own seamless curricula.

A survey concerning the changing of instructional methodologies due to the TCP process was conducted among thirteen tech-prep consortiums in Ohio. Findings from the survey are shown in Table 4.1.

Figure 4.2. School-to-Work Articulation: Interaction Model

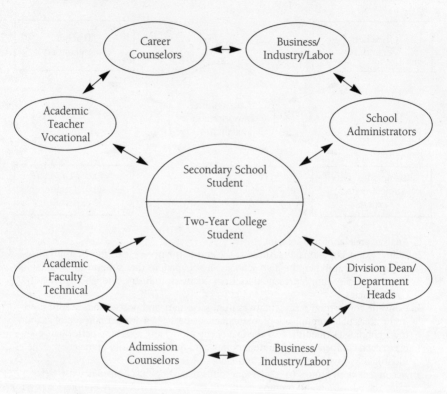

In the last two years, eight of the thirteen tech-prep consortia in Ohio have signed new articulation agreements. The following are the areas that were included in these agreements on a recurring basis, in descending order of frequency:

1. Identifying secondary courses or competencies for which postsecondary credits will be granted toward a certificate or degree or that will allow students to skip prerequisite or introductory courses at the postsecondary level.
2. Working with secondary partners to identify a sequence of required and elective courses or competencies at secondary and postsecondary levels to create a four-year program of study.
3. Defining or changing the content or competencies covered in secondary courses that are part of an occupational sequence.
4. Changing the content or competencies covered in postsecondary courses that are part of an occupational sequence to eliminate gaps or duplication.
5. Providing for joint or exchange teaching involving secondary and postsecondary instructors.
6. Granting advanced standing in apprenticeship programs based on secondary school program completion (Management of America, Inc., 1995).

Table 4.1. Findings from a Survey of Tech-Prep Consortia

$N = 13$

In what courses are instructional methodologies being changed?

Courses	Percentage
Secondary Math	75
Secondary Science	71
Secondary Communications	50
Postsecondary Mathematics	38
Postsecondary Science	29
Postsecondary Communications	38
Secondary Vocational Instruction	54
Postsecondary Technical Instruction	25

Source: Management of America, Inc., 1995.

Table 4.2. Results of Interviews Concerning Implementation of a Seamless Curriculum

Is a "seamless" secondary-postsecondary curriculum being implemented in your consortium?

Representative	Percentage Yes
Local high school district ($N = 22$)	32
Joint vocational ($N = 22$)	41
Two-year college ($N = 24$)	58

Source: Management of America, Inc., 1995.

Interviews were conducted with twenty-two Ohio local school district representatives, twenty-two joint vocational school representatives, and twenty-four community and technical college representatives concerning implementation of a seamless curriculum. The results of the interviews are shown in Table 4.2.

The data in Table 4.2 reveal that secondary and postsecondary representatives are aware of the seamless curriculum concept and are working toward implementing this concept in their tech-prep consortium model. Obviously these data were captured at an early stage of tech-prep development in the state of Ohio. As their five-year plan progresses, the figures in Table 4.2 should increase on a yearly basis, with a goal of implementing a 100 percent seamless curriculum throughout Ohio tech-prep consortiums by the year 2000.

The ultimate benchmark for the tech-prep process is quite simple. Does the implementation of a seamless curriculum help the high schools deliver a better-prepared student to the two-year colleges? Of equal importance will be whether the two-year colleges can deliver a better-prepared student to our four-year colleges and universities.

College and University Articulation

Most existing tech-prep and school-to-work articulation agreements have been developed between local school districts and two-year colleges. Community colleges already have long-standing articulation agreements to support the matriculation process into four-year colleges and universities according to their stated mission (Hammons and Maignan, 1995).

Recent tech-prep and school-to-work legislation creates an opportunity for all two-year colleges to strengthen their relationships with their local colleges and universities. A 2 + 2 + 2 articulation ladder concept has been developed and utilized by many institutions. This concept means students take two years of high school, two years at a two-year college, and the final two years at the college or university level. This model allows students to enter and exit the program at any point in their career. It also allows a wide variety of options at the two-year college level. Students may initially enroll in job training programs and continue their education until they attain an associate degree that is transferable to a college or university.

The Process

Although there are no set procedures for developing articulation agreements between two-year colleges and senior institutions, many colleges and universities require the following items during the articulation process.

Institutional Articulation Agreements. These serve as a contract or binding agreement between two institutions which describes the specific conditions that are guaranteed to students and graduates of a two-year college as they transfer to a specific four-year college or university. Generally this document addresses issues related to guaranteed admission, admission criteria, class rank, and student rights and privileges. Institutional articulation agreements vary and should be read carefully for a complete understanding of the conditions related to transferring from a two-year college to a specific four-year institution.

Usually, institutional agreements deal with the admissions process at the senior institution. They also describe the benefits entitled to a person enrolling with junior status. These agreements *do not* guarantee graduation for every student in two years. Institutional agreements do not address curriculum issues. These agreements basically state that senior-level administrators at both institutions (usually presidents or chancellors) agree in terms of formulating articulation agreements. After these agreements are signed, program areas can begin developing specific articulation agreements (Paynter, 1996).

Program Articulation Agreements. Individual program articulation agreements include a very specific breakdown of the course work that should be taken at a two-year college, not only to obtain the associate degree but also for maximum transferability into a specific baccalaureate completion program at the four-year receiving institution. Program articulation agreements also indicate the courses students must complete to obtain a bachelor's degree once they transfer to the receiving four-year institution. This document becomes a curriculum road map for students to view all their course requirements. Specific questions concerning the interpretation of this document should be directed to the admissions office of the four-year receiving institution.

Program agreements are fluid and need to be reviewed annually to reflect any curriculum changes made in the past school year. Community colleges and four-year institutions have full-time staff to address these issues. Others, such as two-year technical colleges, need to address this critical staffing issue as their articulation agreements increase due to tech-prep and school-to-work initiatives (Paynter, 1996).

Industry Training and Apprenticeships. Two distinct models exist for articulation agreements with business and industry: training and formalized apprenticeship programs.

When dealing with less structured industry training programs, one model for articulation purposes is an individual studies degree program. The associate degree in technical studies in Exhibit 4.2, for example, is ideal for customized training programs and apprenticeship training programs. This program allows a student the flexibility to combine key elements of several technologies in a meaningful and logical way. This is accomplished under the guidance of a technical studies council composed of appropriate administrators and faculty. The technical studies council helps the student formulate a course of study that closely matches his or her goals and needs. The course of study is committed to writing, and upon successful completion of the program, the student is awarded the associate of technical studies degree.

The second articulation model at the postsecondary level deals with formalized apprenticeship training programs. In this model, the company's apprenticeship program is developed utilizing courses within a preexisting degree program, such as tool-and-die technology. The students follow the institutional guidelines for the degree program, but two distinct options exist in the apprentice program:

1. The courses may be offered on a flexible schedule that does not meet traditional college time lines.
2. Students may be granted credit for field experience or other education courses, which allows for the reduction in the amount of time required to receive a degree.

The maximum amount of credits to be transferred into this program due to field experience or other education experiences varies by institution.

Conclusion

Articulation, as presented throughout this chapter, is more than isolated articulation agreements between high schools, two-year colleges, and colleges and universities. It is a comprehensive statewide plan involving all levels of education. Recent federal tech-prep and school-to-work legislation encourages the development of a seamless contextual learning curriculum from high school through the associate degree, with a natural extension to the baccalaureate degree.

As many of the tech-prep and school-to-work consortia throughout the country mature and students complete their associate degrees, it is expected

Exhibit 4.2. Example Associate of Technical Studies Program

DIVISION OF ENGINEERING TECHNOLOGY
ASSOCIATE OF TECHNICAL STUDIES
MANUFACTURING STUDIES and
SKILLED TRADES TECHNOLOGY MAJOR

The Technical Studies program for the Manufacturing Studies and Skilled Trades Technology Major has been developed to serve students who have completed or plan to complete an apprenticeship training program in the North Central Technical College Division of Corporate Services, or who have completed an apprenticeship training program elsewhere that is approved by the college. Any student may seek the Associate of Technical Studies Degree, Manufacturing Studies and Skilled Trades Technology Major, who meets the following criteria:

1. Is or has been enrolled in an apprenticeship training program in the Division of Corporate Services or has completed an approved apprenticeship training program elsewhere that is approved by the college.
2. Satisfies the general admission requirements of North Central Technical College.
3. Has submitted his/her apprenticeship training program of studies and evidence of successful completion of an approved apprenticeship training program.
4. Prepares and submits the Technical Studies application proposal.
5. Develops a course of study with the assistance of the Chair of the Technical Studies Council which meets the academic requirements of the program and which is acceptable to the Technical Studies Council.

ACADEMIC REQUIREMENTS

This Technical Studies program will follow the same curriculum structure as other degree programs. However, the program of studies (outlined in the following pages) has the following academic requirements, and the curriculum plan must contain the following:

1. A minimum of 21 credit hours of general courses, including:
   a. Twelve (12) credits of communications, including ENG 108 Speech or ENG 109 Interpersonal Communications.
   b. Nine (9) credit hours of general electives, at least one course of which must be in the humanities area and one course in the social science area.
2. A minimum of 23 credit hours of basic courses, including:
   a. At least two courses in mathematics.
   b. At least one course in physics.
   c. Four (4) credit hours in ENR 195 Engineering Programming and three (3) credit hours in ENR 265 Engineering Economics.
3. A minimum of 48 credit hours of technical courses.
   a. Forty-five (45) of these credits are awarded for completion of an apprenticeship program approved by the college.
   b. Technical elective courses to complete this requirement must be approved by the Dean of Engineering.
4. A minimum of 100 credit hours.

Source: North Central Technical College (Mansfield, Ohio) Catalog, 1995–1996.

that more and different articulation agreements will evolve. Two-year colleges are the focal point for the development of these articulation agreements. Continued support services will need to be available for those institutions that request assistance in the development of articulation agreements to support the involvement of apprenticeship programs, business, industry, and labor.

References

ERIC Clearinghouse on Adult, Career, and Vocational Education. *Tech Prep Questions and Answers: Information for Program Development* (IN364). Columbus, Ohio: ERIC Clearinghouse on Adult, Career, and Vocational Education, The Ohio State University, 1996.

Hammons, F. T., and Maignan, G. "A Status Report on the Established Articulation Agreements to Support Florida's Statewide Tech Prep Initiative" [http://sun6.dms.state.fl.us/flstw/tpaind.html]. Oct. 1995.

Management of America, Inc. "An Evaluation of Tech Prep in Ohio: Year One Final Report." Tallahassee, Fla.: Management of America, Inc., Nov. 1995.

Paynter, S. *Transfer Guide to 4-Year Colleges and Universities.* Mansfield, Ohio: North Central Technical College, May 1996.

U.S. Department of Education. School-to-Work Web site. [http://stw.ed.gov/factsht/bull 1196.html]. Nov. 1996.

DAVID A. JUST is dean of corporate and community services at North Central Technical College, Mansfield, Ohio.

DEWEY A. ADAMS is professor and coordinator of general occupational education at North Carolina State University, Raleigh, North Carolina.

This chapter presents two case studies with extensive statistical data on the effectiveness of the partnership approach for student employment.

The Role Community Colleges Should Play in Job Placement

Laurel A. Adler

Community colleges and secondary schools have traditionally tended to see themselves as responsible only for the classroom aspects of school-to-work systems, with little obligation to play any role in job development or job placement. But to ignore the role that community college educators can and should play in assisting students who are moving into work and career areas is to ignore the reality of the changing workplace and the stronger accountability measures that are advocated in school-to-work systems. Community colleges can be effective in providing job development and placement services, either directly or in partnership with other agencies within a school-to-work system.

This chapter describes various existing partnership models in which schools and community agencies work together to ensure that training actually results in jobs. The chapter also discusses the interconnectedness of economic development and job training and placement. The most recent economic downturns in the U.S. economy and labor market have taught us that it is not enough just to provide job training, hoping that the jobs for which we have prepared students still exist. Educators must be able to identify future careers and train for those broad-based skills that will meet the needs of the labor market of the future. This chapter describes various successful models that not only work to stay ahead of the job market but can actually assist in the creation of new and additional jobs within the community through partnerships with business and industry. The chapter also describes specific strategies in job development and job creation that could be adapted in other communities.

Education and Economic Development

It has been widely documented that the income disparity between the rich and the rest of American society has been steadily widening for more than two decades. A broad range of policies has been proposed to reverse the trend. However, what has been less apparent is the strong parallel between the economy of the 1990s and that of the 1890s. A century ago the average American family was still struggling to cope with the economic dislocations engendered by the Civil War and the Panic of 1873, which had combined to reverse nearly thirty years of growing equality of wealth and the rise of a middle class. Income distribution had become radically skewed. Immigrants crowded our major cities, competing for work with hordes of native-born farm laborers made jobless by advances in agricultural technology.

To be sure, the oncoming scientific revolution was already in evidence. But it was a future many feared rather than welcomed. People were apprehensive that only a wealthy elite would benefit from the new technology, while the masses would be reduced to poverty. In the 1890s no one foresaw a society needing automobile assemblers, machinists, flight attendants, X-ray technicians, punch-press operators, airframe mechanics, drywallers, or a host of other occupations that did not exist then but that are in demand now. Today, however, the manufacturing jobs that brought prosperity to so many are disappearing, going the way of nineteenth-century farm labor.

Students now need to develop both broader and deeper skills in order to meet new competitive standards and to complement flexible organizational structures and technology (Carnevale, 1989). Drucker (1994) describes the current trend as moving toward what he calls the "knowledge-based society," where more and more skills will be needed and will need to be updated on a lifelong basis. The competitive workplace of today, regardless of the product or service, is an environment designed around technology and highly skilled people working as part of a much larger whole. A student's total educational experience is now an important predictor of successful job placement and advancement. Thus educators, by default, have become the initiators of successful career paths.

Since many educators have limited experiences in business and economic development and job development, in order for these new approaches to be successful, community colleges must learn to partner with other agencies (both businesses and other public agencies) to deliver the entire educational package. Where these partnership approaches to education are successful, data show that program graduates go into higher-paying jobs than students who have had classroom training alone. In addition, surveys of business partners have indicated that many of these jobs were actually created by employers to provide jobs for students with whom they had developed a mentoring relationship prior to the students' completing their education, and for whom they had developed a sense of responsibility.

Model Projects

The first three projects described here are among fourteen core studies conducted by the Academy for Educational Development (AED) in 1995, under contract with the U.S. Department of Education. The final two models have extensive follow-up data, which is described in greater detail.

Oregon Youth Transition Program. The target population of this statewide program is youth with disabilities. The project is a collaborative partnership among the Oregon Department of Education, the Oregon Vocational Rehabilitation Division, the University of Oregon, and public school districts. The goal of the partnership is to provide a menu of services to students, while they are still in school, to help them make the transition from the classroom to employment. While the initial strategies were developed to assist the disabled population, elements have now been expanded to serve the general population of students.

Key to successful job placement is the role of the "transition specialist," who is responsible for coordinating recruitment of students, student assessment, developing individualized plans, developing job placements, and supervising students on-site. The transition specialist functions as part of a team that provides information and support to instructors, students, and potential employers (Rogers and Hubbard, 1995, pp. 72–73).

Kalamazoo Valley Consortium Education for Employment Program. The Kalamazoo, Michigan, program is a school-to-work partnership of the community college, nine school districts, and major businesses in the county. The partnership pools its resources to furnish staff above and beyond the classroom teachers to provide job development services to students. A key feature of this program is the use of unpaid internships, in which students get early firsthand knowledge of the demands of a real workplace. This strategy also allows for high student visibility with potential employers and creates a linkage between workplace and classroom instruction, and paid employment at the same site or in a related industry. The partnership network of colleges, schools, and businesses allows for a sharing of resources and access to job development services that no one school or college could provide on its own. The Kalamazoo program has been particularly effective in helping to prevent students from dropping out of school. The AED report on student response to the program indicated that students who participated in the program were more encouraged to remain in school and had modified their career goals because of the program (Rogers and Hubbard, 1995, pp. 60–61).

Baltimore Commonwealth. The Baltimore Commonwealth is a partnership between the city's business and education communities and government that provides employment training and placement services to the city's youth. The Commonwealth utilizes the "one-stop" approach by consolidating services from many agencies and businesses under one roof. There also are offices located at each of Baltimore's high schools and community colleges, which are staffed by youth coordinators who recruit students, match them up with available services, and help with job development and placement. A key strategy used by the Commonwealth is student "career clubs." These clubs offer career counseling and instruction on specific "job-getting" and "job-keeping" skills (Rogers and Hubbard, 1995, pp. 54–55).

Baldy View Regional Occupational Program. The health careers program offered through the Baldy View Regional Occupational Program was developed to meet the needs of health industry employers in the southern California area. Adults and secondary students are enrolled in health careers courses in addition to taking on-campus academic classes. Students receive college credit through tech-prep agreements with several local community colleges. The classroom serves as a laboratory where student practitioners are engaged in simulated activities that closely parallel the kinds of activities the students would perform at the work site (Weigel, 1996).

Unpaid work-site training is an essential link to subsequent paid employment. After students achieve the required classroom-based competencies, they are placed in a business site (hospital, medical center, and so on) for an unpaid internship. Personnel at the work site become mentors and teach the student specific competencies identified in their individualized training plans. Students are monitored at their training work site by the instructor, who assesses their training and discusses their progress with work-site mentors. After completion of the unpaid work-site internship, instructors and the work-site supervisor help the student obtain paid employment.

Program follow-up data revealed the following:

1. *High school graduation rates.* A significantly larger proportion of students who completed the health careers program graduated from high school, compared to students who received no work-site-based occupational education.

2. *Postsecondary enrollment.* Of the students in the follow-up study, 76.5 percent continued their education and were currently enrolled in college, compared to 56.9 percent of general education students.

3. *Employment after graduation.* There was a significant difference in the rate of employment between students who had completed the program and those who had no unpaid work-site-based occupational training. Among students who had completed the Baldy View program, 86.3 percent were employed two years after completing the program, compared to 58.8 percent for the general education students.

4. *Salary differences.* Of those students who had completed the health careers program, 53.7 percent were earning $8 to $13 per hour; only 22.6 percent of general education students were earning that wage.

5. *Job advancement.* Over half (51 percent) of the students who had completed the health careers program had received a job advancement, compared to 11.8 percent among those who had not completed the program (Weigel, 1996).

East San Gabriel Valley Partnership. This partnership in East Los Angeles County is composed of four community colleges; fourteen school districts;

three California state universities; the University of California, Riverside (UCR); and over three hundred businesses and community agencies. The community is composed predominantly of ethnic minorities. Hispanics are the largest ethnic group, at over 65 percent of the population.

The model utilizes several key components directly related to job placement:

1. *A combination of instructional approaches.* These include classroom instruction, unpaid work-site learning, community service learning, paid work experience, integrated academic and vocational instruction, peer tutoring, community mentors, and job shadowing.

2. *Cooperative partnership programs.* There are currently over three hundred partnership agreements between businesses and the partnership, and project instructors develop new business partnerships on an ongoing basis. In addition to unpaid work-site instruction, business and industry volunteers provide mentoring, job shadowing, and job placement opportunities for students.

3. *An individualized learning plan for each student.* Included in this plan are the specific academic skills and job-related competencies each student needs to achieve proficiency in his or her training program. Specific support and follow-up services needed to help students make the transition into employment are identified and provided.

4. *Tech-prep articulation agreements.* The partnership's 2 + 2 and 2 + 2 + 2 tech-prep articulation agreements allow the student to apply course work completed at the secondary level to program requirements at the community college and state university.

5. *Accessible, ongoing support services.* These are provided in cooperation with community agency partners, which offer services to help students overcome barriers to school completion and job placement, including job shadowing, child care, and transportation to work sites.

6. *Program evaluation.* The California Education Research Cooperative (CERC), the educational research wing of UCR, supervises a multiyear student follow-up program. A recent follow-up study using paired control groups to analyze follow-up data over a five-year period identified several significant findings:

- *Partnership students are more likely to graduate from high school.* Partnership students had significantly better graduation rates than the control group.
- *Partnership students are more likely to be employed.* The employment rate for partnership students was consistently above 90 percent, while the control group's rate of employment ranged from 57 to 85 percent. Both male and female partnership students were significantly more likely to be employed full-time than were their counterparts in the control group. Over 90 percent of the partnership students were employed full-time, while only about 40 percent of the control group held full-time jobs.
- *Partnership students are more likely to get upwardly mobile jobs.* Over 16 percent of the partnership students studied were classified as being in a management

track, while only about 4 percent of the control group were clearly in management track jobs.

- *Partnership students are more likely to pursue higher education and are more likely to have a higher grade point average upon graduation.* Two other statistically significant outcomes that may have had an effect on job placement were the higher rates of postsecondary enrollments for partnership program graduates and their significantly higher ending grade point averages, despite their beginning with the same grade point averages as their matched-pair counterparts.

Based upon these evaluation results, UCR researchers have theorized that placement in upwardly mobile jobs related to training seems to be improved when an educational program works closely with business and industry. By utilizing a wide variety of community and other resources, the model is a cost-effective one that can be replicated in most communities throughout the United States.

Common Elements of Successful Models

While the successful models described above are each unique in many ways, there are some common elements to all of them, regardless of their location and administrative structure. These common elements include the following:

- They are organized as partnerships.
- They utilize resources from a variety of agencies and businesses.
- They use unpaid work-site learning opportunities and business-based classrooms.
- They offer transition activities from unpaid work-site learning experiences to paid jobs.
- They have staff specifically designated for job development.

Setting Up Job Placement Partnerships

In his analysis of Business Education Partnerships, UCR researcher James Dick notes that for partnerships to be effective in training and placement, educational leaders must promote a shared vision of student learning, support a sense of ownership and responsibility for student successes through inter- and intra-organizational communication, and foster a sense of mutual gain ("win-win") by understanding how different partners benefit and celebrating the successes of each (Dick, 1993).

The following basic steps to developing successful job placement partnerships are based on the concepts described in the above models. They place high priority on interagency partnerships and on utilizing unpaid work-site learning activities as a vehicle to successful job placement. These steps can be followed by individual instructors or by staff designated specifically for job development.

Coordinate the business and educational factors. Identify your needs, the job training program area, the number of students involved, geographical locations, where the jobs and work-site learning opportunities are in relation to your campus, and transportation options.

Assemble application and implementation materials. Before contacting a business to request an unpaid work-site learning position, assemble all of the forms and materials required to promote the student. These documents would include course outlines, to explain what the student has learned; letters of introduction; work-site agreements for affiliation; on-the-job supervision report forms; and student progress reports.

Contact area businesses. After an initial telephone contact, make a personal visit to the business to explain the program and its benefits, and leave copies of the program guidelines. In order to maintain an ongoing source of business contacts, it is beneficial for program coordinators to participate in community affairs and for volunteers to speak at chambers of commerce and service clubs.

Match students to appropriate work-site locations. Match the skills, interests, and future career goals of students as closely as possible with the available work sites. Identify the student you would like to place in a given work site and explain the qualifications of the student to the work-site supervisor.

Visit the work sites. Instructors or job developers should visit the work sites on a regular basis to observe students in action at the work sites and to meet with students' work-site supervisors.

Maintain business partnerships. Partnerships between educators and businesspeople have to be continually nurtured, and typically it is the educators who must make the greater effort to maintain communications.

- Be available for phone calls, or return calls promptly.
- Show appreciation to business partners by, for example, sending thank-you letters; presenting organizational plaques for professional support; organizing recognition breakfasts, luncheons, or dinners; arranging for newspaper coverage of businesses' contributions; including site supervisors on college advisory panels; or inviting businesses to be guest speakers in classrooms or at staff development meetings.
- Ask for the professional input of business partners, to infuse business expertise into the curriculum.
- Keep business partners informed of educational, operational, and scheduling changes.

Facilitate students' transition to paid employment. Frequently a student's unpaid work-site learning experience evolves into paid employment. Having personally trained them, business volunteers develop a vested interest in the students they mentor. Consequently, when a job opens at a participating business, the student participant's chances of getting it are good. A work-site learner is a "known quantity," as opposed to a stranger walking in the door.

Sometimes the business will feel so positive about a student participant that it will actually create a job for him or her. However, even if a student's unpaid work-site learning does not turn into a paid position, the student will nonetheless have a recent reference and up-to-date skills, which are powerful tools in job placement.

Conclusion

By partnering with businesses, community agencies, and other schools, community colleges can successfully meet the challenges of the new economy and labor market. Postsecondary education can no longer take place just within the four walls of the college classroom. By utilizing businesses as living classrooms, students gain the skills, confidence, and resources they need to move easily from education to careers. Job placement thus becomes a natural last step in the educational process, and it is easily achievable through collaborations among all stakeholders—the student, the school, and the business community.

References

Carnevale, A. *Training America: Strategies for the Nation.* Alexandria, Va.: National Center on Education and the Economy and the American Society for Training and Development, 1989.

Dick, J. *Business/Education Partnerships: What We're Learning.* Riverside: California Educational Research Cooperative, University of California, Riverside, 1993.

Drucker, P. "The Age of Social Transformation." *The Atlantic Monthly,* Nov. 1994, pp. 53–80.

Rogers, A., and Hubbard, S. *Cross-Site Analysis.* Washington, D.C.: National Institute for Work and Learning, Academy for Educational Development, 1995.

Weigel, L. "Selected Differences Between General Education High School Students and High School Students Who Completed an ROP Health Careers Program." Unpublished doctoral dissertation, University of La Verne, La Verne, California, 1996.

LAUREL A. ADLER is superintendent of a regional occupational program in West Covina, California.

The authors present a model for a workplace mentoring program, including highlights of exemplary plans and an evaluation instrument.

Workplace Mentoring: Considerations and Exemplary Practices

Carl Price, Claudia Graham, Janet Hobbs

Since passage of the Carl Perkins Act in 1990 and the School-to-Work Opportunities Act in 1994, *mentoring* has become an academic and workplace buzzword. In work-based learning, mentoring refers to a plan designed to cultivate a career-enhancing relationship between a youth and an experienced employee assisting with the youth's school-to-work transition. Mentoring provides guidance to inexperienced employees embarking on their careers. Generally it includes a formal, structured program established by an organization to foster a career-oriented, role-model relationship between a businessperson and a student or new employee, and it often continues on an informal basis once the structured program is completed. In school-to-work mentoring, a third person is also involved—a representative of the college or school, who provides necessary information on the program and obtains feedback.

Role of the Community College in Mentoring

The community college maintains an interest in workplace mentoring because of its mission to provide broad-based training for specific jobs. To help ensure the success of their graduates, community colleges must not only offer job-specific training, they must also offer students guidance in adapting to different organizational environments, including their structure, culture, and ethics. Many community colleges throughout the United States recognize these needs and are strengthening the role of mentoring in school-to-work programs. For example, in western Pennsylvania, the Southern Alleghenies Tech-Prep Consortium has obtained a $75,000 federal grant "to train school- and work-based mentors." Additionally, in Eugene, Oregon, Lane Community College has received funds to "serve as a mentor for school-to-work leaders in at least five other states" ("Community Colleges Chosen as Mentors," 1996, p. 3).

Community college workplace mentoring programs, such as cooperative education, apprenticeships, and internships, generally establish three-way partnerships between the student, the employer, and the college. This three-way relationship benefits everyone involved: the college gains professional and technical feedback concerning its training, the employer gets a temporary employee at a reduced cost and has the opportunity to hire an employee with experience who has already been assimilated into the workplace, and the student gains valuable experience. As a result of feedback received from employers, graduates, and students, Wake Technical Community College (in Raleigh, North Carolina) has instituted a program it refers to as the "capstone" project, which emphasizes the importance of team-based problem solving and interpersonal communication skills. The capstone project requires students in their last quarter to work in teams of three to four students to complete a curriculum-based project that integrates their general education and their technical skills. Industry professionals and faculty evaluate the project; thus the college receives feedback on the overall preparation of students for the technological workforce. Other North Carolina community colleges have already expressed an interest in adapting the capstone concept on their campuses.

In addition, since the community college and the workplace will become vital partners in welfare-to-work programs, systems must be established to address not only job-skills training but also the acculturation of employees into organizations. One way to accomplish these goals is through community college and business alliances, which will enrich the mentoring process. However, the concept of workplace mentoring goes beyond the college educational experience. Since only a limited amount of workplace mentoring occurs at the college level, the concept must be continued once the student becomes an employee.

Workplace mentoring, whether for full-time employees who have completed their education and training or for high school and college students participating in work-based learning programs, requires formulating a plan, implementing it through establishing a mentor-mentee relationship, and evaluating it. Formulating a mentoring plan not only helps inexperienced employees understand their job and their workplace, it also produces a lasting relationship with the mentor. This chapter highlights exemplary mentoring programs, presents a workplace mentoring model, and provides a generic evaluation instrument for the overall plan. The model provides initial guidelines for starting a workplace mentoring plan, one that will ensure a new employee's success in his or her company.

Exemplary Work-Based Learning Programs with Mentoring Components

Mentoring has emerged as an important part of such work-based learning programs as apprenticeships, cooperative education, internships, and other partnership programs. Many mentoring plans, whether elaborate or informal, have been implemented in both large Fortune 500 companies and smaller companies throughout the United States. Highlights of selected companies with exemplary programs involving a mentoring component follow:

1. IBM emphasizes six "global mentoring principles" in its companywide plan. The mentoring process may differ from division to division, but the principles remain constant:

- The employee is the driving force behind a mentoring relationship.
- Mentoring is all-inclusive and addresses the needs of a diverse population.
- Mentoring is an enabling process that facilitates career development and skills exchange.
- The mentor and the mentored employee are mutually committed to a beneficial mentoring relationship.
- Mentoring is based on a commitment of trust and confidentiality between participants.
- Management is committed to a mentoring-rich learning environment.

Alan Outlaw, an engineer at IBM in Raleigh, North Carolina, who hires engineering technology co-op students from Wake Technical Community College, begins introducing co-op students to IBM with an orientation. Human resources personnel conduct the first orientation; next, Mr. Outlaw follows up with an orientation to his area, which includes explaining job duties and reviewing a checklist to answer questions about the facility, security, and parking. Then the students are "assigned to a technician to guide them through the job and acclimate them to the team and to workplace habits." Since the team work concept is encouraged, co-op employees are invited to attend team meetings and area meetings. Outlaw believes the co-op students "get a better perspective of the total development part of the organization and see how their work fits in and the end result" (A. Outlaw, personal interview, May 1, 1996).

2. Motorola participates in several programs that use mentoring as one aspect of the company's workforce development commitment. In Austin, Texas, Motorola has established partnerships with other members of the Greater Austin Chamber of Commerce in support of the school-to-work transition. Motorola Austin believes that "Austin's young people deserve to be nurtured. Mentored. Encouraged. Challenged. Exposed to exciting career opportunities. Instilled with dreams. And shown the pathways to help transform dreams into reality." The school-to-work transition program supported by Motorola and other businesses "involves building systems that connect learning with workplace opportunities." In addition, the Texas Alliance for Minorities in Engineering (TAME) works to encourage "minority and female students to enter engineering fields and helps equip them with the skills necessary to succeed" (internal Motorola company document ["Inspiration Through Education"], 1995). According to Sharon Knotts Green, external education manager at Motorola Austin,

Companies partner with a school and meet with the students in a TAME club format at least once a month. During these monthly sessions, students learn about Motorola's business operations, discuss interviewing skills, write resumes, and hear presentations on various aspects of college or work life. The program culminates with the hiring of eligible juniors and seniors during the summer. The purpose of mentoring high school students does include acculturation to the organization. For the TAME program, the primary purpose is to teach students the full range of skills that will be needed to become successful in engineering. Mentors have helped students evaluate colleges, learn how to study for a particular course, and dress appropriately for work [personal interview, 1996].

The goal of Motorola's Career Pathways Program, begun as a pilot program during the 1994–95 academic year, is to move "Motorola's work-based learning programs closer to a workforce development strategy," according to Green. "In this respect it differs from TAME, because it is designed to give students a work-based learning experience in an immediate area of business need." The results of the project after the first year of operation are encouraging. Citing the ways in which students benefited from the program's emphasis on both life skills and work skills, Green said, "Some tremendous relationships were formed. In one case, a mentor helped her mentee purchase a used car. Another mentor whose mentee was a teenage mother enjoyed sharing baby care strategies. In all of the five lasting mentor-mentee relationships, I had the impression that the entire department or small group mentored the student, not just the person assigned. Based on this experience, I now speak in terms of a department mentoring students in the workplace" (personal interview, 1996).

3. AETNA Incorporated, based in Hartford, Connecticut, established project STEP-UP, "a mentoring program initiated through a business/education partnership." Started in 1985, the program helps disadvantaged teens "make the transition successful from school to work." AETNA employees who serve as mentors "are expected to offer personal counseling, help with homework, and act as role models" (Stern and others, 1994, p. 58). After graduating from high school, most of these students gain full-time employment at AETNA.

4. Eastman Chemical Company includes cooperative education and summer job opportunities in its Partnership Model program. According to Betty DeVinney, manager of Eastman's employment, "Our management must be involved on a personal level—involved in the recruiting effort and involved as mentors (Nabours, 1994, p. 57). Eastman provides co-op and summer students with an orientation that includes details on the job they will perform, the training they will receive, and the evaluation they will receive.

5. Southern California Edison (SCE) started its job skills partnership program in 1990. Today the utility company continues to work successfully with at-risk high school students, providing them with workplace experience. High school juniors and seniors "are paired with journeyman mentors for a full year, experiencing six-week rotations in maintenance, operations, administration,

warehouse, and technical occupations" (Ingles, 1994, p. 28). Ingles notes that the goals of the program include "students learning essential skills" for the transition from school to work, "creative problem solving, effective listening techniques and oral communication, negotiation and teamwork and other workplace skills" (p. 28). SCE employees willingly volunteer to be mentors, and those selected provide students with a written performance appraisal at the end of each six-week rotation. The mentor, student, and high school counselor meet to discuss the appraisal and what the student learned during the six-week period and to plan for the next rotation. Mentors typically involve students in troubleshooting on-the-job problems and in a variety of work-related meetings. By 1994, of the 113 students who had participated in the program, 94 percent had graduated from high school. Many went on to technical, community, or four-year colleges; others got jobs.

6. Workbound—a partnership between 120 local businesses and five Sheboygan County, Wisconsin, high schools—has provided mentors to more than two hundred students. Workbound was created in response to complaints from businesses that students were unprepared for the workplace. Career counseling is one of the most significant aspects of Workbound. It begins during a student's sophomore year and leads to a job in the student's area of interest during the summer before his or her senior year in high school (Johnson-Elie, 1995, p. 1). In addition to exploring careers, students are encouraged to set personal goals aimed at developing healthy lifelong learning habits.

One important common denominator in these programs is the significance of the mentor-mentee relationship—many of these relationships continue to thrive long after formal mentoring ends. For example, one former student mentee at Motorola who ran out of money for college "contacted his former mentor, who helped him obtain part-time employment, thus qualifying the student for Motorola's tuition reimbursement program" (Green, personal interview, 1996). Other commonalities include fostering team building and enhancing problem-solving skills. These companies are attempting to meet the needs of their new employees, whether they are full-time or are participating in one of the various school-to-work partnerships.

While many companies endorse mentoring principles, there is not always clear evidence that the broad principles are formally tailored to the specific workplace. For mentoring to be successful, it must be adapted to the needs of a unit, department, or division within an organization. The model depicted in this chapter is generic; therefore, it can be tailored to most workplace settings to assist a new employee.

Mentoring Plan Components

A successful mentoring program consists of program design, mentor and mentee development, and evaluations, all of which are equally important and integrated. These components are summarized in Exhibit 6.1.

Exhibit 6.1. Mentoring Plan Components

Program Design

- Establish program goals and objectives
- Develop a process to identify mentors
- Develop training for mentors
- Determine the length of the program

Mentors' Responsibilities

- Orienting mentees
- Observing mentees' work performance
- Acclimating mentees into team concept
- Communicating with mentees, both interpersonally and in writing
- Evaluating mentees
- Formulating professional development plans with mentees

Mentees' Responsibilities

- Immersing themselves in the company
- Accepting feedback from mentors
- Developing the necessary skills for the job
- Demonstrating the ability to work within the corporate culture
- Formulating a professional plan that incorporates short- and long-term goals

Evaluation

- Evaluating the program
- Evaluating the mentors
- Evaluating the mentees

Program Design. Program design consists of four tasks:

Establishing Goals and Objectives. The first step in developing a mentoring program involves determining the goals and objectives for the program as they relate to the business or industry. Broadly speaking, the primary goals of a mentoring program are to provide guidance for inexperienced employees to successfully start or advance their careers and to assimilate new employees into the workplace culture. To achieve these broad goals, a mentoring program must satisfy the following three objectives:

1. It must contribute to the mentee's successful orientation and adaptation to the workplace and the specific job.
2. It must provide role models for the cultural integration of the employee into the workplace.
3. It must promote team-based communication.

Achieving the primary goals and objectives requires a holistic approach, integrating the total person into the workplace and its systems. It therefore goes beyond fine-tuning job skills for the specific position to include acculturation into the organization and to the team approach to problem solving and communication.

Identifying the Mentor. One of the most important steps in the mentoring process, following the establishment of the program's goals and objectives, is to select and train the mentor. The employees selected to participate in and lead such a program not only must have the education and job skills necessary to guide and advise a new employee but also must understand the nuances of the company's culture and workplace ethics.

An employee who experiences an intensive mentoring program under the tutelage of a competent mentor will become an asset to the organization and will ideally become a role model for future employees. Therefore, the mentor must be an experienced employee, someone who demonstrates a commitment to the mentoring activities that will enhance the experience for both the mentor and the mentee. Specifically, the mentor should be familiar with the mentee's job, thoroughly immersed in the organization's structure and culture, and proficient in interpersonal and communication skills. These skills will ensure a positive relationship with the mentee and assist in acclimating the new employee to the company. Employees mentoring students who are participants in work-based learning programs have an additional responsibility: they will need to understand "the school-based learning component that complements [the program]—in particular the academic and technical curriculum design (Brustein and Mahler, 1994, p. 31). In short, a mentor should be a seasoned employee who can help an inexperienced employee on the job and within the organization. In many ways, the mentor is a person "who acts as a counselor, adviser, and professional guide to a less experienced person in the same organization" (Carter, 1994, p. 51).

Developing Training for Mentors. Experienced employees need training prior to serving as mentors to new employees, especially if they will be mentoring in school-to-work programs. That training generally includes written guidelines, checklists, and evaluation instructions. In essence, a successful mentoring program must provide formal written guidelines for all involved. Mead Corporation, a producer of paper and other forest products as well as a leader in electronic publishing, maintains a highly structured cooperative education program that includes training for supervisors "to help them learn how to develop assignments, to evaluate performance, and manage employees" (Love, 1992, p. 13).

Determining Program Length. The length of the mentoring program depends on the complexity of the job, the level of the position in the organizational structure, and the work experience of the employee. The maximum time allotted for most formal mentoring programs varies, although six months is perhaps the longest. In the Multiple Engineering Cooperative Program (MECOP) at Oregon State University, which in 1993 involved thirty-one companies, evaluation occurs twice: the first at three months, and the second at the conclusion of a six-month co-op assignment. "These evaluations are conducted by both the intern's company mentor and the MECOP program administrator" (Barnett and Petersen, 1993, p. 28). It seems reasonable to assume that young, inexperienced employees will need three to six months in a formal mentoring program, whether it is part of an internship, a cooperative education program, an apprenticeship, or a first full-time job.

Mentors' Responsibilities. The mentor's role involves orienting the mentee to the company, both to the physical organization and to its human resources. The initiation into the organization follows the orientation conducted by human resources personnel. The mentor first provides an understanding of the physical plant and the resources available to employees. For example, the mentee should become familiar with the types of computers and software used as well as their accessibility to the employee, have a working knowledge of the organizational structure, be introduced to the personnel responsible for benefits information and plant maintenance, and understand any issues regarding parking, transportation, safety, and security. Typically these areas are covered in an initial broad-based orientation. However, the mentor should review each of these as the need arises and train the mentee to use company resources to answer common questions concerning company practices.

The mentor-mentee relationship involves distinctive roles for each individual. The mentor builds a personal relationship with the mentee in order to develop a communication style with which both are comfortable. The mentor and mentee schedule formal and informal meetings to build their relationship and create a professional development plan for the mentee that will accomplish the objectives of the program. Fostering team interaction and communication requires an initiation period for the new employee to become acquainted with colleagues and peers. The mentor and team peers communicate team goals, which are usually related to the company's mission, to the new employee.

The mentor should be familiar with the mentee's job in order to observe and evaluate the mentee appropriately. To advise the mentee on performance expectations, the mentor should observe the mentee both formally and informally. Observation times allow the mentor to assess how the mentee performs the job, relates with others, operates in a team environment, and solves problems. Based on these observations, the mentor then guides the mentee into developing objectives that will help build strengths and overcome obstacles.

Mentees' Responsibilities. By definition, the mentee is new to the organization or position and therefore will need to gain insights into the functioning of the organization with guidance from an experienced, competent mentor. For the mentoring relationship to be successful and for the mentee to accomplish the program goals, the mentee must show commitment to the mentoring process. Accepting advice and guidance and then following through on suggestions for improvement are keys to a successful relationship. This entails verbal and written communication. The mentee must show a willingness to spend extra time gaining knowledge of the company and its products by reading annual reports, the employee handbook, and material concerning innovations. The mentee will perform the job to meet or exceed company standards and will ask questions and engage in problem solving as necessary to complete the task. Demonstrating competence in job performance is essential to the mentee's workplace assimilation.

Besides commitment, the mentee must also demonstrate an understanding of the corporate culture, including appropriate social and business behavior. The corporate culture can be described, in part, as the shared attitudes and practices that have become the accepted mode of behavior among the company's employees. For example, many new employees are unaware of how to address supervisors, whether by first name, last name, or title. In some organizations, an employee's immediate supervisor may prefer to be addressed by first name, while those above expect to be addressed by title and last name. The formal practices, such as dress codes, expected of employees are generally written in the employee handbook. Perhaps the most significant responsibility for the mentee is to demonstrate commitment to the process.

Evaluation. The evaluation component involves all participants in assessing one another, as well as the overall effectiveness of the program.

1. The mentoring program should be evaluated periodically by each participant to determine its effectiveness. The mentor should evaluate the program and the mentee. The mentee should evaluate the mentor.
2. The evaluation should include separate assessments of all component parts of the mentoring program.
3. The company may want other participants, such as supervisors, to evaluate the program.

An instrument using a Likert-type assessment will offer the opportunity to measure the degree of success of each program component (See Exhibits 6.1, 6.2, and 6.3). An analysis of the data will assist in making decisions about future changes in the program. The sample evaluations below offer a starting point for organizations to begin the assessment process. The evaluation of each component should not be limited to these statements. Each organization or subunit will most likely add more specific statements tailored to their specific needs.

Conclusion

Mentoring programs are an effective way to integrate inexperienced employees into the workplace. In order to implement the mentoring process, a plan

Exhibit 6.1. Program Evaluation

Based on your perception, rate the following items using the following scale: 1=Strongly Disagree, 2=Disagree, 3=Neutral, 4=Agree, 5=Strongly Agree	1	2	3	4	5

Program

1. The process to identify mentors was adequate.
2. The length of the mentoring program was adequate to accomplish the goals.
3. The training for mentors was adequate and helpful.
4. The guidelines for the mentoring process were available.
5. The guidelines for the mentoring process were helpful.

Exhibit 6.2. Mentor Evaluation

Based on your perception, rate the following items using the
following scale: 1=Strongly Disagree, 2=Disagree, 3=Neutral,
4=Agree, 5=Strongly Agree   1   2   3   4   5

Mentor

1. The workplace orientation was beneficial.
2. The mentor provided adequate feedback following his
   or her observations.
3. Ample time was allowed to observe the mentor.
4. Adequate opportunities were provided to participate in
   team meetings.
5. The company's style of written communication was
   explained.
6. The company's style of verbal communication was
   explained.

Exhibit 6.3. Mentee Evaluation

Based on your perception, rate the following items using the
following scale: 1=Strongly Disagree, 2=Disagree, 3=Neutral,
4=Agree, 5=Strongly Agree   1   2   3   4   5

Mentee

1. The mentee demonstrated an adequate
   understanding of the company and its products.
2. The mentee demonstrated an acceptance of feedback
   from the mentor by making appropriate changes.
3. The mentee demonstrated appropriate job skills.
4. The mentee's verbal communication skills are
   appropriate.
5. The mentee's written communication skills are
   appropriate.
6. The mentee is capable of working independently.
7. The mentee makes appropriate use of company
   resources.

integrating the four major components—program design, mentors, mentees, and evaluations—must be formalized and implemented. The key to a successful mentoring program is to establish a positive relationship between the mentor and mentee. To determine the success of the program, an evaluation becomes crucial to ensure that appropriate changes and revisions occur as necessary.

References

Barnett, P., and Petersen, G. "Engineering Better Graduates." *Journal of Career Planning and Employment*, 1993, 52(4), 27–29.

Brustein, M., and Mahler, M. *AVA Guide to the School-to-Work Opportunities Act.* Alexandria, Va.: American Vocational Association, Nov. 1994.

Carter, T. "Mentoring Programs Belong in College Too." *Journal of Career Planning and Employment,* 1994, *54*(2), 51–53.

"Community Colleges Chosen as Mentors." *Community College Week,* 1996, *7*(9), 3.

Ingles, P. "Electric Avenue." *Vocational Education Journal,* 1994, *69*(3), 28–30.

Johnson-Elie, T. "School-to-Work Program Earns National Praise. *Milwaukee Journal Sentinel,* June 22, 1995, Business Section, p. 1.

Love, R. "A Winning Proposition: Mead's Technical Co-op Program." *Co-op Experience,* 1992, *3,* 11–13.

Nabours, N. "Competitive Advantage Starts and Ends with 'Quality.'" *Journal of Career Planning and Employment,* 1994, *55*(1), 6–7, 57.

Stern, D., and others. "Mentoring Programs." *Research on School-to-Work Transition Programs in the United States.* Berkeley: National Center for Research in Vocational Education, University of California, Berkeley, 1994.

CARL PRICE is executive vice president of Wake Technical Community College in Raleigh, North Carolina.

CLAUDIA GRAHAM is head of the college transfer department at Wake Tech.

JANET HOBBS is head of the English department at Wake Tech.

Exemplary apprenticeship programs in community and technical colleges have recently received considerable interest that has rejuvenated both youth and adult programs. This chapter considers both the attributes and characteristics of nine exemplary apprenticeship programs.

The Apprenticeship Revival: Examining Community College Practices

Ann V. Doty, Robin T. Odom

Since 1917 the United States has endorsed vocational education programs, which have been supplemented significantly in recent years by the Carl D. Perkins fund. The Perkins Act has distributed funds primarily to disadvantaged or special needs students; it was not intended as a primary source of support for high school or college graduates seeking employment. The Department of Labor has also developed programs that increase the skills of youth and adults, with a direct impact on their marketability. The current focus on apprenticeship demands quality programs that include national, competency-based skill standards supported by industry.

New technologies and a global marketplace have resulted in a new workplace that requires skilled workers who can readily adapt to change. Colleges are facing the dilemma of providing more effective services in an era of decreasing revenues. One solution has been the development of strong partnerships between educational institutions and industry. The apprentice programs surveyed for this chapter illustrate how successful collaboration can generate the following productive outcomes:

- Coordination between secondary and postsecondary educators and programs
- Integration of academic and vocational or technical curricula
- Interaction with industry personnel during curriculum development and program evaluation
- Opportunities to provide specialized courses using industry resources that otherwise would not be offered

- Keeping college personnel current with emerging technologies and industry trends
- Utilization of industry equipment and staff for teaching purposes

What Is a High School or Youth Apprenticeship?

The Clinton administration has recently placed major emphasis on youth apprenticeships as a strategy for solving the school-to-work transition problem. Youth apprenticeships, for students age sixteen or older, can be defined as an employer-school partnership that integrates academic instruction, structured vocational training, and paid work-site experience. These programs enable high school students to receive on-the-job training, classroom instruction, a high school diploma, and an approved certificate of competency. Completion of a youth apprentice program can lead to entry in a related postsecondary program, an adult apprenticeship program, or permanent employment.

The definition of adult apprenticeship also integrates a structured work experience with a minimum number of hours per year of related or theory-based instruction. Adult programs are custom designed to prepare apprentices for specific careers. Hours spent in related instruction can be credits earned in a degree curriculum, while work experience hours in a curriculum are applied to the requirements of the apprenticeship credential. At the completion of the program, the adult apprentice may earn an associate in applied science degree or a four-year degree in addition to a nationally recognized, portable apprenticeship certificate.

High school or youth apprenticeship programs are designed to articulate with adult apprenticeship programs. Articulation is a cooperative partnership process that involves high schools, community colleges, state departments of labor, and industry. Articulation efforts facilitate continuity and coherence in a student's education from one level to another without delays, duplication of courses, or loss of credits.

Expanding Opportunities and High School–Community College Involvement

Historically, apprenticeship programs have been blue-collar programs. The onset of school-to-work funding in many states to supplement and expand tech-prep programs has led community colleges and public school systems to modify administrative codes within their state boards of education. Changes, when approved, permit the expansion of creditable work experience carried out within a registered apprenticeship. Colleges are exploring expansion of curriculum credits. Conditions permitting this expansion of credits include the following situations:

1. The work experience meets certain requirements for work experiences previously authorized by the state board.

2. The student is enrolled under a specific associate degree curriculum program that has its own title, code, and description and meets state regional curriculum standards, based, when possible, on emerging national skill standards.
3. The work experience is included in an apprenticeship plan registered with the state's department of labor.

This model permits the educational institutions to collaborate with the employer and the state department of labor field representative to design a program of study that includes a general education core and a selection of courses that can be independent of any existing curriculum. Apprentice programs are custom tailored to meet the business needs of the sponsoring employer, the career interests of the apprentice, and the approved apprenticeship standards of the registering agency.

Key Characteristics of Youth and Adult Apprenticeship Programs

Alternating parallel periods of campus education and educational work experiences are designed collaboratively with the employer, the educational institutions, and the state department of labor representative. Related instruction, the theory component of an apprenticeship program, can be part of the requirements for a tech-prep or associate degree, associate in applied science degree, or bachelor of science degree. Under the school-to-work guidelines, apprentices are usually registered with the state department of labor, and evaluation of their work is a joint responsibility of the employer and the high school or community college. Work experience contact hours completed in a youth program accrue cumulatively to the work experience hours required in an adult apprenticeship.

Typical characteristics of key programs are that they are based on industry needs and have ample planning time. Wayne Rowley, at the Craftsmanship 2000 apprenticeship program in Tulsa, Oklahoma, started the program six years ago when industry projected a shortage of machinists by 1995. After working closely with the local chamber of commerce for two years, Rowley designed the program to eventually provide work-based opportunities for all students. After two years of planning, the first class started in 1992, before the passage of the School-to-Work Opportunities Act in 1994.

The Nature of Exemplary Programs

Exemplary apprenticeship programs are continually updated and measured against the latest benchmarks in the education and labor arenas. When Gerald Pumphrey, director of workforce preparedness at Guilford Technical Community College in Jamestown, North Carolina, establishes an apprenticeship program, new educational benchmarks, such as those under development for the national skills standards, are incorporated in the program design. Their program curricula have ongoing changes and interface with other transition programs such as cooperative education. Rowley warns that initially programs can be expensive, especially if apprentices are paid or reimbursed for time spent in the classroom. As the Craftsmanship 2000 program has matured, apprentices are now only paid for time spent working at the job site during the summer months.

Barry Blystone, director of training and development of Siemens Corporation in Raleigh, North Carolina, facilitates an apprenticeship program in electromechanical manufacturing and has aligned classic adult and youth apprenticeship programs in collaboration with Wake Technical Community College in Raleigh, North Carolina, and East Wake High School. In 1993 the company planned the apprenticeship program and began development of the curriculum and the instructors. For students, the Siemens program includes preemployment training and a technical skills curriculum. For teachers, the program provides tech trainer development, a two-week paid summer employment opportunity for teachers, work-site visitations by academic as well as technical faculty, and training in math and language workplace applications.

According to Don Williams, dean of vocational and technical education at Rock Valley College, Rockford, Illinois, students in the youth-to-adult manufacturing apprenticeship programs apply in their sophomore year and are selected in the summer prior to their junior year. As juniors, they work ten hours per week at the tech-prep academy; as rising seniors, apprentices work nine weeks in the summer, rotating between seven companies. At the end of the summer the students select three companies where they would like to work during their senior year. The companies concurrently select students for hiring. As seniors, they work twenty hours a week in the apprenticeship program, using an alternating two-week schedule: one week devoted to structured classroom education, either at the academy or in college, and the next week at the company. Table 7.1 provides additional information about the apprentice programs examined by the authors.

Changes in Programs

Changes are most likely to occur as apprenticeship programs increase in size or scope or as a result of program or course content evaluations. Programs continue to grow despite cuts in vocational funds, schedule revisions, and changes in administrative leadership.

For example, the youth apprenticeship program in Beaufort County, North Carolina, has grown from one high school and employer to three schools and fourteen employers. Due to funding cuts and schedule changes, students who are unable to obtain instruction in required classes may attend classes at Beaufort Community College. High school apprentices may enroll in community college classes when courses needed for their program are not offered at the secondary level.

Table 7.1. Characteristics of Exemplary Apprenticeship Programs

Employer and Educational Institution	Time to Develop Program	Criteria to Enter Apprenticeship Program	Percentage of Students in College Tech-Prep or Co-op Education	Type of Training	Apprentice/Student Evaluation Methods
National Spinning/Beaufort Community College (NC)	12 months to develop and 6 to design work plan	1. Referrals based on related courses in trade 2. Adult basic education test for math and reading level as prescreening for program	n/a; offered to all juniors	machine operator	employer every 6 weeks gives grade for work component plus VOCATS at beginning and end of school year
General Motors/GASC Mott Community College (MI)	26 months	minimum 9th grade reading level, "C" or better in algebra, attendance, ability to graduate on time from high school, interested in manufacturing	75 percent	manufacturing-technical careers-skilled trades	oral, written, performance test, take the UAW/GM national apprenticeship test
GASC (MI)	evolved over time	no set standards, look at National Skill Standards	75 percent	health care	same as above
Bosch Power Tool Corp/ Craven Community College (NC)	24 months	grades, references, work assessment, employer interview	n/a	tool and die maintenance/mechanics	oral, written, performance test
AMP, Burckhardt America, Newman, K & C Machine Co./Guilford Technical Community College (NC)	12 months	grades, attendance, participation in tech-prep, program application	100 percent	machinist	oral, written, performance test

Table 7.1. (continued)

Employer and Educational Institution	Time to Develop Program	Criteria to Enter Apprenticeship Program	Percentage of Students in College Tech-Prep or Co-op Education	Type of Training	Apprentice/Student Evaluation Methods
Dow Corning/Guilford Technical Community College (NC)	12 months	grades, attendance at summer metals companies, enrolled in college tech-prep program	100 percent	chemical process manufacturing	same as above, including higher-level math, science, and communications
Nations Bank/Guilford Technical Community College (NC)	12 months	scholarship-level grades, attendance, workforce development coursework, job shadowing	100 percent	banking/finance	same as above
Guilford Technical Community College (NC)	12 months	grades, attendance, commitment to college tech-prep curriculum	100 percent	automotive technology	same as above, ASE certified
Blum, Daetwyler, Sarstedt, Timken, Ameritech, Accuma/ Central Piedmont Community College (NC)	12 months or less	varies, based on GED, high school diploma, cumulative GPA, DOL mechanical aptitude tests, personal interest, references, interview, referral from high school apprenticeship director, participation in tech-prep course of study, employment by one of six participating employers	not known for some students yet, but a growing percentage for others in emerging school-to-work programs such as tech-prep or cooperative education	manufacturing engineering technology, machinist, graphic arts, administrative office technology, construction trades, food service	employer, DOL, self-evaluation, written, math and English performance tests, co-op learning objectives, position given by employer

Atwood, Elco, Rockford Spring, Ingersoll, Plauter-Maag, Header Die & Tool (charter companies)/Rock Valley College (IL)	approx. 12 months	must be in 10th grade, cumulative GPA of 2.0 or higher, successful completion of algebra I, good attendance, and good attitude scores	many participate in tech-prep initiative	health careers, financial services, metalworking (toward 6 two-year degree programs)	most of the above to be considered for two-year scholarship
Craftsmanship 2000 (representing multiple employers)/Tulsa Junior College and Tulsa Technology Center (OK)	24 months	entrance requirements include grades, attendance, references, and an application to the program	currently not tracked, but there is coordination with tech-prep curriculum	metalworking	academic/technical teachers evaluate and forward to job site mentor for further evaluation, then conference
Siemens, Inc./Wake Technical Community College (NC)	ongoing	all above plus "0" drug test tolerance, teacher interview, pass algebra I	100 percent	electrical-mechanical	performance

During a recent period of growth, Sandra Lare, at Central Piedmont Community College in Charlotte, North Carolina, began to coordinate the college's apprenticeship program with its work-based learning, cooperative education program. The original program was a joint venture by the Charlotte Chamber of Commerce and the college, but now the college has full responsibility for program operation. Larger, comprehensive programs benefit from having a point person to manage the variety of processes occurring simultaneously.

Susan Richvalsky coordinates programs at the Genessee Area Skill Center (GASC) tech center in Flint, Michigan, where the apprenticeship programs have changed in three ways. First, the entrance requirements for student selection have been increased. In order for students to be able to pass the UAW/GM apprenticeship test above the national average, students must enter, for example, with a reading level above the 9th grade to successfully complete the reading comprehension section. Second, the curriculum is often modified. Richvalsky calls it a "living document" that experiences major changes every summer. As employers have been added to the partnership, their needs have resulted in changes to the curriculum to adequately prepare students for their work experiences. Third, as school-to-work programs become institutionalized, transition programs such as apprenticeships and tech-prep programs have promoted reorganization of both schools and businesses to accommodate these integrated efforts. Tech centers like GASC have reorganized to eliminate traditional administrative positions. More personnel are being hired from the private sector to bring education and employers together to provide these programs.

With rapidly expanding programs in manufacturing and engineering technology at Central Piedmont, George Timblin, head of the engineering and advanced technology department, cites the need for coordination with businesses at the college level and regular communication to handle program details—from recruitment to testing to registration and other transition processes involved in admissions, introduction to academic and technical departments, and student service areas. This coordination means that employers can assume that their employees will move with ease between work and education arenas.

While Pumphrey at Guilford and others in North Carolina anticipate rapid development of apprenticeship programs in the areas of electrical, textile, furniture, and culinary trades, there is consensus that advancement of these programs by industry and community colleges drive the need to implement national skills standards in areas where none previously existed. The Craftsmanship 2000 program, not unlike Richvalsky's experience at GASC, has changed to require applied math and science courses that went beyond the scope of courses offered in the original tech-prep curriculum. One factor that prompted this change in the Craftsmanship 2000 program was a 25 percent dropout rate of apprentices in the first year of operation. Currently they are losing less than 10 percent of their apprentices.

In the machinist program at Craven Community College, New Bern, North Carolina, David Bauer, of the business and industry services department, has worked to change the college's policy toward awarding college credit for coursework through a credit-by-exam policy. Previously no course credits were available to students enrolled in the regular and advanced machinist programs. These examples demonstrate how apprenticeship programs continue to evolve and grow as a result of improvements made to meet the needs of employers, students, and schools.

Advice to Practitioners Considering Apprenticeship Program Development

Collaborative efforts between departments of labor and educational agencies, along with the dedication of space and personnel by all partners, has both rehabilitated the old image of apprenticeships and broadcasted the usefulness of apprenticeship programs as vital to educational reform in schools and colleges. Survey respondents indicated that flexibility is required for successful development and growth of youth and adult programs.

The educators who responded to the survey emphasized the positive influence of a program that is industry-driven and based on the needs of the employer. Community colleges are especially responsive institutions to their communities. It is crucial that all parties have support from the top stakeholders, superintendents, company and college presidents, and others in top posts.

Wayne Rowley strongly feels there is never too much planning for apprenticeship programs. Developers of the Craftsmanship 2000 program spent two years looking at the theoretical aspects of the program. The process of developing the subsequent partnership, trust levels, and ability to learn from one another requires time. Strong leadership (with vision and passion) is needed, and the benefits to all parties must be shared up front. Attitudes, reservations, and turf issues must be addressed as quickly as possible. The need to sell every layer of the program to players and participants is essential. Initiation by a strong businessperson respected in the community is helpful to program development.

Once a program has been started, strong monitoring is a key to a successful apprenticeship program. Most of the surveys indicated that schools, colleges, and businesses should stay involved and track students, maintain contact, and make each student feel that he or she is part of a larger community, not just another body on campus. Program managers should link programs to students before they reach postsecondary experiences. Survey respondents also suggested that credentials are a concern, especially where state funding is predicated on full-time student enrollment status. Consider that the student and the business are the customers, and focus on their satisfaction with the whole experience. Be careful with personnel changes. Have the organizational leaders reinforce their commitment to the apprenticeship program. Look more closely at instructor credentials, how they develop curricula, and whether or not they actively use applied learning methods or alternate delivery methods.

Lare and Timblin at Central Piedmont have words of wisdom to apprentice coordinators. They ask that coordinators

- Understand the role of the postsecondary institution in such an adventure and ensure that high school–community college coordination is a priority.
- Develop a model that combines the best resources in education and business so that there is a keen market focus.
- Unite school-based and work-based training.
- Meet with participating employers regularly, and provide, if possible, a workplace mentor—and even provide training for the mentor or supervisor.
- Provide constructive feedback to students on a regular basis.
- Find resources to enhance marketing, student recruitment, and program maintenance.

According to Gerald Pumphrey, it is essential to link apprenticeship programs, tech-prep processes, and national skill standards where possible. The Piedmont Triad Center for Advanced Manufacturing (PTCAM), Greensboro, North Carolina, has played a major role in its school-to-work collaboration with the Guilford County schools to create a comprehensive program that truly links partners in academic and skill training. Concurrently, Don Williams, at Rock Valley College, Illinois, states that challenges exist to retrain teachers and counselors, change the educational criteria for new teachers, improve program curricula, and gain acceptance of secondary student work by colleges—all components of tech-prep reform. Successful programs must have established individualized career plans for students, have sufficient work-based sites, and be linked with regional economic development plans. With better-prepared students exiting high schools, postsecondary institutions will need to provide challenging curricula.

Conclusion

There remain several issues that community colleges face with youth-to-adult apprenticeship program sequences. The issue of allowing credit for job-site work experience and learning will continue to need attention. Teacher credentials, at both the colleges and job sites, may require increased certification to meet technological advances in industry. Development and standardization of program curricula will supplement articulation opportunities. Evaluation methods must also be standardized to ensure portability of apprentice skills. Coordination issues abound, from support staff for apprentice programs to the provision of instruction at job sites and linkage of secondary and postsecondary schedules. Other concerns include class scheduling to meet the needs of small as well as large businesses and providing insurance coverage at both levels of apprenticeships.

Colleges must consider innovative methods to address shortages of personnel and funds to develop, promote, coordinate, and evaluate programs. In the Illinois Rock Valley program, a temporary staffing personnel agency arranges student placement in five hundred apprentice jobs, without charge. New industries that have traditionally not been associated with apprenticeship programs should be invited to participate with groups that have successful programs. Most importantly, changing attitudes and perceptions of apprenticeship training follow on the heels of well-administered programs.

Despite the above issues, apprenticeship programs in the educational arena have the advantages of reducing expenditures for up-to-date technology, integrating industry needs into academic learning experiences, linking workplace practices to curriculum revisions, and promoting communication between secondary and postsecondary staff.

Apprenticeship programs foster community involvement. This involvement is generated either by meetings of countywide chief executive officers; by reflection groups that involve parents, educators, and employers; or by industry-related needs. Students and parents are responsive to the high level of requirements and usually react positively to the new ways of using knowledge. Schools have upgraded how they deliver information, often thanks to systemic reform efforts initiated by federal tech-prep funds. Shared resources, a result of increased articulation between secondary and postsecondary systems, have become essential in apprenticeship programs. Finally, use of the nonprofit model (where no partner receives financial gain) has helped avoid the politics and budget struggles commonly found in educational systems.

Most survey respondents included statements, such as George Timblin's, that educators should remember that employers are their customers. Employers control resources, and companies such as Siemens have verified the gain in long-term job training savings. When developing a program, load the effort into the front end or the beginning of the project. When successful apprentice experiences are maximized for the employers, the programs can then grow, have perceived academic and work experience value, and be more attractive to students and parents.

Working partnerships, networking of companies, informed career selections, college opportunities, and the resulting well-trained workforce are the rewarding results of these efforts. Successful partnerships, like those surveyed, triangulate activities as equal partners. These programs are three-dimensional, living organisms that generate benefits, when managed with care and in light of benchmark practices that are easily reproducible.

ANN V. DOTY is a coordinator for tech-prep programs in the North Carolina Community College System.

ROBIN T. ODOM is a representative for the North Carolina Department of Labor Training Initiatives Division.

This chapter presents a no-excuses approach to career development in the community college that connects school-to-work partners with a student-centered focus.

Quality Emphasis on Career Development and Continuous Self-Improvement

Joe A. Green, Phyllis A. Foley

Drawing together school-based and work-based learning practices to connect fragmented elements, individuals, and institutions requires a systematic and collaborative framework. In a school-to-work system, guiding youth and adults through the processes of career development and continuous self-improvement becomes everybody's job. School-to-work systems present unparalleled leadership opportunities for community college counselors and career development specialists. Quality initiatives in business, industry, and education provide a superb framework for that leadership.

Quality initiatives have played a major role in revitalizing and transforming countless American businesses and industries into high-performing work organizations. Regardless of the model that is most popular at the time, names like Total Quality Management, Continuous Quality Improvement, and Quality Corporate Culture find their roots in W. Edwards Deming's management philosophies, which catapulted Japan into manufacturing and technological leadership (Walton, 1986).

As tech-prep and school-to-work programs and other business-education linkages promote quality initiatives, community colleges adopt quality models to improve program effectiveness and customer service. Quality models generally share the common elements of insistence on quality; teamwork and participatory management; customer focus; seeking and fixing faults in the system; and continual education and training. Each element presents a key to successful involvement of community college counseling and career development personnel in school-to-work systems. This chapter will explore new directions

NEW DIRECTIONS FOR COMMUNITY COLLEGES, no. 97, Spring 1997 © Jossey-Bass Publishers in community college career development from the perspective of these hallmarks of quality initiatives in a school-to-work context.

Insistence on Quality

Insistence on quality is critical to quality initiatives' establishing a no-excuses standard for delivery of quality products and services. The quality-oriented community college benchmarks quality standards for its career development program and works collaboratively to achieve each standard.

The task of benchmarking for quality in career development involves adopting external standards of excellence and developing internal needs-based standards. External standards may be based on state or national standards developed by membership organizations' policy boards, or on exemplary practices identified in other institutions.

The *National Career Development Guidelines: Local Handbook for Postsecondary Institutions* (National Occupational Information Coordinating Committee, 1989) provides a national standard for practice and a sequential plan for program development. The collaboratively developed handbook establishes benchmarks for development of the adult learner's self-knowledge, educational and occupational exploration, and career planning as a phase in a lifelong process. The handbook offers more than standard setting by outlining a process for planning and development of a comprehensive career development program.

Recent research by Cunanan and Maddy-Bernstein (1995) identifies exemplary career guidance programs in high schools and colleges. In their summary of program highlights, the researchers focus on various program components, including career guidance and counseling program plans; collaboration, articulation, and communication; and institutional support, leadership, and program evaluation.

Descriptions of exemplary programs provided by Cunanan and Maddy-Bernstein (1995) include listings of national or state guidelines utilized as program standards. Various colleges, including San Joaquin Delta College in Stockton, California, and Renton Technical College in Renton, Washington, base their programs on the National Career Development Guidelines developed by the National Occupational Information Coordinating Committee (1989). In addition to adopting the national guidelines, these colleges base their programs on statewide system guidelines for student matriculation and targeted populations.

North Harris College, near Houston, Texas, responding to an identified need to improve awareness and vertical communication between area high schools and the college, developed the Shared Counselor Program. Through the Shared Counselor Program, rather than volleying blame between institutions for barriers to communication, each high school in the service area shares a counselor with the college. Each shared counselor devotes four days per week to the high school and one to the college. While on the college campus, the shared counselor participates in a full rotation through each college counselor job role (Stanfield, 1995).

Teamwork and Participatory Management

The college that is serious about achieving high-quality benchmarks builds teams to get the job done. Teamwork, collaboration, and participatory management promote shared responsibility for quality performance and reduce tendencies for fragmentation and redundancy. The teamwork process brings together people and programs in the college and extends outward, to create connections with the community.

A high-quality program can unify the array of often disconnected counseling and career development services at a college. College personnel serving students in programs for remediation and development, disabilities services programs, gender equity programs, programs for single homemakers, welfare reform programs, and programs for economically disadvantaged individuals become active members of the counseling and career development team. The team, which also involves faculty and administration representatives, meets frequently to plan and implement quality initiatives in counseling and career development.

Just as the college's counseling and career development team harnesses the power of the college to support students, collaboration between the college and the community taps broader resources to the benefit of students, the community, and the college. The college actively contributes to the success of collaborative initiatives in the community, such as "one-stop career shops," tech-prep programs, school-to-work systems, welfare reform, and workforce development programs.

The quality-oriented college uses a variety of tools to facilitate collaborative initiatives with the community. The Education for Tomorrow Alliance bonds Montgomery College with the Conroe (Texas) Schools, area chambers of commerce, and local businesses in a partnership to enhance career development and learning experiences of area students from elementary school through college. The alliance sponsors mentorships, internships for students and instructors in area business and industry, and a variety of other initiatives for building students' competence, self-esteem, and decision-making capabilities.

Kalamazoo Valley Community College, in Kalamazoo, Michigan, provides leadership within partnerships, engaging the college with area public schools and business to improve students' work habits and skills and educational preparation for work, beginning in elementary school (McCauslin, 1993).

Columbia State Community College in Columbia, Tennessee, and Volunteer State Community Colleges in Gallatin, Tennessee, participate with human service agencies in Career Links, a shared technology project. Career Links helps agencies develop a technological one-stop career shop to reduce redundancy in client data collection and to improve timely service delivery. Pellissippi State Technical Community College, near Knoxville, Tennessee, is a key member of a public sector–private sector partnership launching a federally funded school-to-work local implementation.

To date, community colleges in fourteen states have participated in the piloting and implementation of the Counseling for High Skills (CHS) program. The project, developed by Ken Hoyt, Kansas State University, and funded by the DeWitt Wallace Reader's Digest Foundation, provides a computer-based guidance link between high school students and their peers in postsecondary and community college programs. In Tennessee's exemplary implementation of the CHS project, Tennessee's twenty-six technology centers and fourteen community colleges and technical institutes surveyed their students to provide answers to high school students' most asked questions. Student customer satisfaction information on more than three hundred occupational programs will be encapsulated in a CHS computer guidance diskette to be provided with training to one thousand middle and high school counseling and guidance personnel.

New York's Mohawk Valley Community College responded to a need for mentoring support among students in nontraditional occupational programs by recruiting and training college alumni. The alumni mentors contribute to an expanded support system designed to improve student retention and success.

Customer Focus

While teamwork and collaboration in the college and the community expands the college's power to get things done, a clear customer focus is required to effectively channel that robust energy. A college can easily identify a number of different customers to be served. In counseling and career development, however, the student is clearly the primary customer. Indeed, a college that chooses to target the student as its primary customer will also be responsive to the requirements of the other customers in order to equip the student for success in a changing world.

A college focusing on service to the student as its prime customer aggressively works to become a user-friendly institution and to deliver on its promises. The student-to-counselor ratio is too great for the counseling staff to be fully effective in all these activities. Thus it becomes everyone's job to increase ease of access to and utilization of quality educational programs. The college and the community become engaged in addressing the needs of the customer by merging efforts and streamlining overlapping tasks.

The complex task of counseling and career development necessarily involves counselors, faculty, staff, and the community. They cooperate in promoting recruitment, students' personal and academic growth, career decision making, and educational and employment planning.

Tech-prep and school-to-work programs offer excellent vehicles for collaboration in recruiting and meeting the needs of students emerging from the K–12 school system. Through local tech-prep consortia, Tennessee's public technology centers, technical institutes, and community colleges work with hundreds of local schools and businesses to improve students' educational and

employment opportunities through counseling, career development, curricular reform, and articulation.

Pellissippi State Technical Community College in Knoxville, Tennessee,
and the surrounding schools and communities parlayed their successful tech-
prep programs into a broader plan, which resulted in federal funding for a local
school-to-work implementation plan. The plan engages local schools, technology centers, and the college with human service agencies, employers, labor
organizations, students, and families. Working together, they build on early
successes in education and work-site experiences for all students.

Workforce development and welfare reform initiatives offer opportunities
for collaboration targeting underserved adult populations. Dynamic linkages
with agencies charged with serving school dropouts, welfare recipients, displaced homemakers and other workers, individuals with disabilities, and other
special populations produce powerful potential for service. In Lawrence and
Wilson Counties, Tennessee, the Career Links program electronically links
client data among educational and human service agencies. The pilot program,
motivated by high dropout rates when clients were referred to other institutions or agencies, offers a single intake form, streamlined assessment and
screening, and electronic transfer of data, with safeguards for client confidentiality. The community college participants in the program aim to help eliminate the kind of inefficiency that once resulted in an agency's testing one client
forty-six times.

The college that collaborates effectively will experience increased opportunities to serve nontraditional students, including first-generation college students (youth and adult), individuals with disabilities, students with economic
or academic disadvantage, displaced homemakers and other workers, and
older students. Campus traditions and habits often serve to make nontraditional students feel unwanted, uneasy, and at risk of failure.

The college must first realize the rich potential brought to the institution
by nontraditional students and then find ways to improve matriculation rates,
support, and successful program completion for those students. Although community colleges generally maintain open admissions policies at the institutional
level, barriers to program admission—some legitimate and some artificial—
often prevent promising nontraditional students from getting a chance to start.

By employing alternate means for assessment, screening, and selection,
the college can improve the equity of these gatekeeper functions. Portfolio
assessments, performance assessments, and other competency- and experi-
ence-based reviews help reduce the artificial barriers.

The higher education system in Wisconsin completed an extensive collaborative deliberation to produce its competency-based admissions standard.
Similarly, Tennessee Technology Centers and Community Colleges negotiated
an articulation agreement by which technology center diploma graduates can
demonstrate competency on a combined knowledge- and performance-based
assessment to significantly shorten the time required to complete the associate
degree.

Because access means much more than mere arrival on campus, the counseling and career development program must continually link with resources in the college and community to support retention, program completion, placement, and follow-up. Before a student is ready to benefit from career guidance and instructional supports, basic needs like child care, transportation, financial planning, and interpersonal relations often must be addressed.

In proposing to establish a safety net, the counseling and career development program at North Harris Montgomery Community College in Houston, Texas, hopes to create a campuswide effort to accept and support students who may be at risk in the college environment. The Safety Net Program will equip students and their families with information and skills while encouraging faculty and staff to be more accepting and supportive.

The Pathway Program at St. Petersburg Junior College in St. Petersburg, Florida, provides strong career guidance coupled with a comprehensive support system for nontraditional students entering the nursing and allied health programs (Cunanan and Maddy-Bernstein, 1995).

The Career Links program—discussed earlier—in Tennessee's Lawrence and Wilson Counties provides not only ease of access for the client but also a means of rapid response to emerging needs. If a student is repeatedly absent from the educational program, a caseworker can be notified immediately and help find a remedy to a health, transportation, child care, or other barrier.

Seeking and Fixing Faults in the System

As is evident in the discussions above, many community college counseling and career development programs are implementing foundations for continuously improving the quality of their customer service. It remains all too simple, unfortunately, to pat ourselves on the back for these fine examples and to be too easily satisfied, without really achieving quality benchmarks.

A system that insists on quality openly seeks faults in the system, not for blame but for repair. Everyone probably recalls the suggestion box approach, to quietly address flaws or at least allow a harmless venting of frustration. The quality system goes well beyond the suggestion box model. The quality organization invites associates and customers to point out flaws and requires timely response. Tennessee's Roane State Community College, in developing quality standards for itself, continuously seeks and fixes flaws internally and provides Total Quality Management (TQM) training to other educational institutions and to industry.

Continual Education and Training

As flaws and service opportunities are identified, an institution cannot provide a quality response without state-of-the-art knowledge and skill. Thus a primary responsibility of the community college and its counseling and career development program is to stay abreast of current research through continual education and training. Counselors and other student service personnel must assume both the role of student and that of teacher.

As continual learners, counselors need to complement pre-service foundations with a broad range of in-service learning opportunities. In diploma- and certificate-granting technical institutions, counselors are generally required to have completed at least the bachelor's degree in counseling or a related student service field. In associate degree–granting institutions, the counselor is generally required to have completed at least a master's degree in counseling or a related student service field.

Baccalaureate and master's programs tend to offer an identical program to counselors whether they plan to work in K–12 education or at the postsecondary level. Occasionally the student may have an option to select a precollege or collegiate curriculum course. Rarely does a master's degree counselor education program devote more than six semester hours specifically to career development issues. Programs generally address career assessment within a general assessment course. Occasionally the counselor-in-training can select a three-hour career assessment course.

Counselors who become proficient in career development, career assessment, and nontraditional adult service issues generally do so through a combination of formal and informal in-service education and applied experience. In priority setting, budget planning, and calendar juggling, it is important to heavily emphasize continuing educational opportunities. Rich learning and skill development opportunities can be tapped by signing up for local, regional, and national conferences and workshops. While it is important to participate with "job-alike" professionals in counselor-specific activities, it is critically important to participate in other forums offering enriching opportunities dealing with career development and student support issues. These diverse opportunities are accessed through events sponsored by tech-prep, school-to-work, and workforce development programs and the American Association of Community Colleges, the League for Innovation in Community Colleges, the National Tech-Prep Network, and many other organizations and initiatives.

The counselor's role of lifelong learner is balanced by also serving as a teacher, trainer, and team leader. Through tech-prep programs, school-to-work systems, and other workforce development initiatives, the community college counselor accesses opportunities to lead and train other counselors and guidance teams. Leadership opportunities emphasize the importance of a counselor's effort to stay current in knowledge and skills. Tennessee postsecondary counselors who helped collect student survey data for the Counseling for High Skills project are preparing to train others to use the guidance software. Counselors in North Harris Montgomery's Safety Net program are helping train teams to support nontraditional students.

The Challenge

The convergence of school-to-work and quality initiatives creates a unique opportunity for counselors and other career development professionals. School-to-work initiatives open the doors to involving the college and the larger community in a major emphasis on career development and continuous self-improvement. The hope is to improve the opportunity for all youths and adults to gain quality educational preparation and fulfilling and productive careers. Career development professionals have an opportunity to focus the energy of school-to-work initiatives on quality service to each student as the prime customer. The challenge is to grasp the opportunity by setting benchmarks for quality and making it everybody's business to empower each student to achieve success.

References

Cunanan, E. S., and Maddy-Bernstein, C. "Exemplary Career Guidance Programs: Investing in the Future." *Office of Student Services' BRIEF,* National Center for Research in Vocational Education, University of Illinois at Urbana-Champaign, 1995, 7(3), 1–5.

McCauslin, H. *Partners in Workforce Development.* Kalamazoo, Mich.: Kalamazoo Valley Community College, 1993. (ED 358 888)

National Occupational Information Coordinating Committee. *The National Career Development Guidelines: Local Handbook for Postsecondary Institutions.* Washington, D.C.: National Occupational Information Coordinating Committee, 1989.

Stanfield, V. *Shared Counselor Partnership Tool Kit.* Houston, Tex.: North Harris College, 1995.

Walton, M. *The Deming Management Method.* New York: Putnam, 1986.

JOE A. GREEN *is director of the Tennessee Technology Center at Hartsville, Tennessee.*

PHYLLIS A. FOLEY *is assistant vice president for academic affairs at Volunteer State Community College in Gallatin, Tennessee.*

The contextual curriculum offers a new paradigm for instructional delivery and the development of student competencies better suited for today's work environment.

Contextual Curriculum: Getting More Meaning from Education

Les Bolt, Ned Swartz

This chapter presents a brief explanation of contextual learning, why it is important in a school-to-work system, and some ideas on how it can be accomplished. No matter what restructuring model community colleges use, a key tenet is the integration of the world of education and the world of work. Just as there are many different approaches to integration, there are various approaches to realizing contextual learning. It is not crucial that all institutions use the same model or method. It is vital, however, that all community colleges develop a plan for accomplishing contextual learning, since it is this kind of learning that adds value to those in a workplace environment. The addition of workplace value is a key outcome of a school-to-work system.

Contextual Learning: Designing New Instruction for New Times

Varying definitions of contextual learning can be synthesized as follows: contextual learning is learning that occurs in the most effective and natural manner, associating classroom theory with real-world application. Learning occurs most effectively when information is acquired in the context of its natural use. Conversely, education often tends to be overly organized and compartmentalized from work. Furthermore, curricular decisions are made separate from instructional decisions, disciplines are taught in isolation, and students are divided into groups and separated by levels and talents. Contextual learning seeks to reconnect work and education, curriculum and instruction, different disciplines, and students of various levels and talents. In short, contextual learning is a conduit to applied knowledge.

Changing Climates. The nature of work is undergoing radical change. Education and training systems that still prepare students for the antiquated American industrial model, which stresses conformity and continuity, is not well suited for worker needs in this new era. Globalization of the marketplace and the influences of technological innovation have made this mode of learning and business obsolete. The competitive advantage in today's business world is defined by timeliness, customization, constant improvement, and innovation (Carnevale, 1991). Getting to the market first with the best product has become crucial. Organizational structures have been flattened to accelerate the change process, enhance communication, and make organizations more responsive to changing market conditions. Structural change has dissolved middle management and relocated decision making to the production line.

Traditional wisdom passed from parents to their children, however, suggests that one can prepare for a high-wage career only by earning a baccalaureate degree or higher. Actually, only about 20 percent of high school graduates move immediately to college, and only half of those earn a degree within a six-year period (Gray and Herr, 1995). Contrary to the myth that even embarking on a bachelor's degree program helps pave the way to success, recent projections suggest that associate degree graduates, or those completing work-based programs such as apprenticeships or internships, have higher earning potential and lower unemployment rates than those students who enter college but do not complete a four-year degree (National Bureau of Labor Statistics, 1996).

Evolving Organizational Structures: Link to the Workplace. Relocation of decision-making responsibility to frontline staff has created the need for workers with different basic skills than those in previous generations. Technological innovation has made the workplace a more complex environment, making even entry-level positions highly dependent on technical skills. These are more likely to be acquired in an associate degree or work-based program rather than a university environment. Workers without these technical skills face grim prospects in the new work environment (Reich, 1994). In response to new worker requirements, educational systems must stress the integration of academic, technical, interpersonal, and critical-thinking skills. Workers can no longer operate in competitive isolation but must incorporate their skills into larger work units. Workers must not only be highly competent in specific skills but must also have a liberal arts foundation that will allow them to adapt to meet new demands.

The broad-based, integrative approach of contextual learning can prepare workers for the new work environment. Ask students to recall a course, and they will more likely remember the *way* the course was taught, not the details of course content. Learning through the process of inquiry is a more natural way of learning than the mere acquisition and accumulation of facts (McCollum, 1978).

Deriving Content from Context and Process

Traditional curricula tend to be either content-centered or performance- or competency-based. Neither of these approaches, in their traditional use, serves to foster contextual learning. In content-centered curricula, what is to be taught is identified from the knowledge base that forms the discipline. This knowledge base is separated into logical, sequential units, and those units are developed into curriculum guides or text material. Thus math, algebra, geometry, and calculus become separate courses, taught with minimal concern to the articulation of one to the other. An assumption is made that students will make the connections between courses and synthesize overarching concepts that tie the knowledge base together.

In performance- or competency-based curricula, content is derived from the world of work. This content is organized and subdivided, however, into instructional objectives. The objectives are then taught in some degree of isolation, with the assumption that the sum of the parts will add up to the whole (the gestalt). A performance-based curriculum is designed to make sure that all of the prerequisite skills for a particular job are learned; the flaw is that this approach ignores the holistic nature of the real work environment, making performance- or competency-based curricula of limited use to the worker preparing for the new world of work.

Performing a Contextual Task Analysis. A traditional task analysis, common in a performance- or competency-based model of curriculum development, offers a good starting point from which to develop a contextual curriculum; however, this does not provide the holistic component of curriculum construction that a contextual curriculum demands. Commonly used by technical programs in community colleges, the traditional task analysis focuses on identifying duties and tasks that are elements of a job. Duties and tasks are then validated by practitioners, who also prioritize the ranking of tasks. The methodology of traditional task analysis is to divide curricula into smaller and smaller discrete units until they reach a teachable size. On the other hand, contextual curriculum development identifies not only those skills but also the cognitive processes in which those skills are used, and it conducts a trend analysis to identify the direction in which those skills are evolving.

Mind-Mapping Cognitive Processes. It is one thing to learn the principles of accounting in a course; it is quite another to use those principles on a daily basis as an accounting clerk. The way content is used in a job setting is different from the orderly, sequential manner in which it is traditionally taught. Real life, as distinguished from academic life, is a disjointed and disorderly affair. What are the mental gymnastics that an accounting clerk must use on a daily basis? Which skills are used daily, weekly, or monthly? These questions must be answered to identify the cognitive threads that define a job—the culture of that job.

Performing a Trend Analysis. Are accounting clerks doing things differently than they were two years ago? What will they be doing differently next year? What specific skills are related to trends that come and go, and what broad skills can be used over time to transition into new job requirements? Facility in using a particular software package might be important for an accounting clerk, but basic accounting skills would allow the clerk to move on to new software with minimal disruption. In short, today's worker must not only be prepared for today but also must be equipped to change for tomorrow.

Organizing Curricula and Instruction

In a contextual curriculum, content and the process are inseparable. Instructional process should mirror the use of content. Instruction must become as student-centered as possible, and faculty must become more managers and resources and less "fountains of knowledge." Nontraditional delivery methods may not be classroom- or even school-based, and this is not only an instructor problem. The challenge must also be addressed by fiscal administrators who are involved in resource allocation decisions. Indeed, traditional models of assigning faculty workloads and evaluating faculty instruction may have to be scrapped as the realization evolves that the college may not be as important to the learning environment as the community.

Determining the Instructional Pedagogy. Curricular and instructional decisions are often unique to the community college and the resources available. Thus contextual learning activities most often occur at the micro rather than the macro level. It would be impossible, therefore, to give an exhaustive list of examples of contextual curriculum delivery methods. However, the most common forms of curriculum and instructional approaches for contextual learning can be separated into three different delivery models: a stand-alone or self-contained curriculum component, a cross-disciplinary curriculum approach, and an integrated curriculum approach. Each of these models has potential benefits and problems.

Using a Stand-Alone or Self-Contained Curriculum Component. Discipline and course integrity are normally maintained in this model. This is probably the most commonly used contextual approach, because it requires the least disruption to traditional organizational and scheduling patterns. It is also probably the least effective, in that individual disciplines are placed in the context of the world of work, but connections are not made between disciplines. Course content material and activities to be used for instruction and evaluation are drawn from real work settings. For example, preparation for the position of an accounting clerk would include a course in tax law that uses problems and processes identified in a contextual task analysis drawn from real clients as a source. The course would still focus only on the tax law components and would not, for example, explore the estate planning and accounting procedure angles of the problem.

Using a Cross-Disciplinary Approach. A cross-disciplinary approach offers an improvement over stand-alone components in that the traditional boundaries between courses and disciplines are crossed. The curriculum still can be orderly, but subject matter is integrated to accomplish the overarching goals identified in the contextual task analysis. Instructors from several disciplines plan projects that span several courses, disciplines, or semesters. Although administrators find this model attractive because of its minimal disruption to traditional patterns, in many ways this is the most difficult model of contextual curriculum delivery to implement. A cross-disciplinary approach requires the commitment of faculty and academic administrators to joint planning, yet retains the isolationist mode of actually delivering instruction. If faculty are not committed to synchronization, gaps are likely to occur in the delivery. Hence, the intended outcomes may not be met.

In preparing a student to be an accounting clerk, for example, courses in business accounting, tax law, and financial planning could be fused in a project to develop a plan for a small business that maximizes long-term profitability while minimizing short-term tax burdens. The project outline would be drawn from scenarios identified in the contextual task analysis. Instructors would cooperatively plan the approach to the project so that the outcomes of one course would become the necessary inputs for the next course. An alternative would be to block the three courses so that they could be taught concurrently, or in a team-teaching mode, with many smaller outcomes feeding back and forth between the three courses. Faculty members using this approach would need to maintain constant communication, establish clear evaluation mechanisms, and have a constant student base in all three courses, which could be accomplished through block scheduling.

Using an Integrated Curriculum Approach. An integrated curriculum approach provides the most radical departure from traditional practice, yet it may be the most logical approach to contextual learning. In this model, traditional instructional concepts such as courses and disciplines are discarded as limiting factors. Students are simply presented with an educational plan to meet outcomes identified in the contextual task analysis, and the learning plan may or may not include traditional courses and experiences. Instructional methodology includes learning experiences that mirror as closely as possible the actual use of skills as applied in the work world. Teams of faculty representing the different disciplines plan and deliver cooperatively the instruction and directions that students need in order to reach the desired competencies. Skill sets can be divided into smaller components and taught as seminars, or they could be left as larger units and tied to capstone or benchmark activities. Learning activities could include short courses, modules, internships, mentorships, or apprenticeships, depending on the individual student's learning "prescription." Since not all students with the same career goals would have identical programs, career counseling becomes vital. Furthermore, student progress is not measured in courses completed but in competencies achieved. Because of its outside-the-box approach, this model may meet with faculty reluctance and confusion. Moreover, how do you fiscally account for a student's education? What tuition and fees do students pay? How do you allocate faculty time and other resources? How do you count students in terms of full-time equivalent generation? It is these administrative and fiscal limitations that may make this model difficult to implement unless traditional thinking is abandoned and new paradigms are accepted.

A program for our accounting clerk might include an apprenticeship component, supplemented with both direct and self-guided instruction. Program goals and outcomes would be developed from a career counseling center that would take into account the student's talents, prior accomplishments, and career aspirations. Periodic evaluations would be used to identify student progress toward achieving goals and outcomes, as well as to provide opportunities to revise the educational plan as needed.

Evolving Contextual Initiatives. Tech-prep and school-to-work education plans each encourage the integration of academic and technical instruction. Tech-prep and school-to-work programs also stress the articulation (streamlining) of secondary and postsecondary curricula. In addition, the Southern Regional Educational Board's "High Schools That Work" project advocates restructuring high school curricula to give all students a stronger academic preparation, integrated academic and technical skills, and career decision-making competencies. Evidence to date indicates that the project's integrated, contextual emphasis is highly successful in increasing student's scores in the core areas of math, science, and communications (Bottoms and Sharpe, 1996). As these initiatives take hold, the preparation level of students entering the community colleges, and consequently their demands on the system, will impact curricular delivery decisions.

Verifying Contextual Learning

Contextual learning, just like other forms of learning, must be verified. Most learning evaluation procedures fall along a continuum, moving from norm-based at one end to criterion-based at the other. Norm-based evaluation is generally summative in nature and seeks to identify how well a student has fared compared to other students in similar settings. Norm-based evaluation approaches are used more commonly for content-based curricula. Criterion-based evaluation is more formative in nature and seeks to identify the rate at which a student progresses in a series of skills that combine to identify an educational outcome. Criterion-based evaluation is more common in a performance- or competency-based curricula.

Abandoning Traditional Evaluation Methods. Norm-based evaluation is inappropriate in a contextual learning scenario because it is not based on students' mastery of skills but rather on their relative position in a group of cohorts. Likewise, criterion-based assessment is inappropriate for a contextual environment because it focuses on the mastery of individual skills in isolation from each other (the theory being that if students master all of the parts, they will have mastered the whole).

Adopting Authentic Assessment. Several sources have begun to use the term *authentic assessment* to describe a more dynamic evaluation approach

(Hart, 1994; Darling-Hammond, Ancess, and Falk, 1995; Baron and Boschee, 1995). In evaluating contextual learning, the assessment should be consistent with both the content taught and the process in which the learning takes place. For example, it may be inappropriate to use a paper-and-pencil test to measure content that was taught using a team-based, applied methodology. A more appropriate evaluation might be to assess the team based on how well they were able to use the content to solve a complex problem presented to them. If the learning plan included a work-based component, the best evaluation might measure student success in the work setting. The major hurdle in implementing authentic forms of assessment is the difficulty of abandoning traditional modes of thought, old paradigms of instruction and accountability, and traditional fiscal procedures.

Conclusion

Education's closet is full of discarded ideas that were well intentioned but ill timed. Either such innovations offered a solution to a problem that didn't exist, or they did not solve the problem quickly enough and so were discarded. Community colleges must find ways to develop not only a more relevant curriculum but also a delivery system that will prepare students for a dynamic new environment. As the world moves toward a more global economy, both community colleges and students must learn to work smarter if our nation's current standard of living is to be maintained. The implementation of contextual learning can be a key ingredient to the mix of ideas that will foster this new educational paradigm.

References

Baron, M., and Boschee, F. *Authentic Assessment: The Key to Unlocking Student Success.* Lancaster, Pa.: Technomic Publishing, 1995.

Bottoms, G., and Sharpe, D. *Teaching for Understanding Through Integration of Academic and Technical Education.* Atlanta, Ga.: Southern Regional Education Board, 1996.

Carnevale, A. *America and the New Economy: How New Competitive Standards Are Radically Changing American Workplaces.* San Francisco: Jossey-Bass, 1991.

Darling-Hammond, L., Ancess, J., and Falk, B. *Authentic Assessment in Action.* New York: Teachers College Press, 1995.

Gray, K., and Herr, E. *Other Ways to Win: Creating Alternatives for High School Graduates.* Thousand Oaks, Calif.: Corwin Press, 1995.

Hart, D. *Authentic Assessment: A Handbook for Educators.* Reading, Mass.: Addison-Wesley, 1994.

McCollum, J., *The Inquiry Process of Generating and Testing Knowledge.* Santa Monica, Calif.: Goodyear Publishing Company, 1978.

National Bureau of Labor Statistics. *Employment Outlook: 1994–2005.* Washington, D.C.: National Bureau of Labor Statistics, Office of Employment Projections, 1996.

Reich, R. *The State of the American Workforce 1994: The Over, the Under and the Anxious.* Washington, D.C.: U.S. Newswire, 1994.

LES BOLT *is associate professor in the school of education at James Madison University, Harrisonburg, Virginia.*

NED SWARTZ *is associate dean of allied health, business, and technologies at John Tyler Community College, Chester, Virginia.*

This chapter discusses legal and technological issues that must be considered when developing and implementing school-to-work programs.

Legal and Technological Issues of the School-to-Work Opportunities Act of 1994

Donald W. Bryant, Mary P. Kirk

Tying classroom instruction to practice in the work environment is commonplace. Such practice is exemplified by cooperative education, field trips, and similar endeavors. At the postsecondary level, the practice is exemplified by cooperative education, allied health clinical experience, and comparable technical-vocational undertakings. Tech-prep education, school-to-apprenticeship, business-education contracts, and career academies are foundations on which school-to-work systems will be built. The exemplary nature of such practice was recognized in 1994 by the passage of the School-to-Work Opportunities Act, which seeks to not only prepare people for employment and smooth the transition from school to work but also to provide a more solid framework within which such activities may occur.

Yet the School-to-Work Act poses many significant challenges for all parties. One of those challenges revolves around the liability of participation in such endeavors. Laanan (1995) highlights these issues, posing questions concerning a company's legal liability for student trainees, who controls the standards for accountability, and who is responsible for quality. Another challenge involves the use of technology. How will the use of technology impact service-area designations and instructional practices?

Although the discussions of these areas are too complex for a short treatise, some preliminary answers may be provided here. It is hoped that the reader will use this material as a basis for further exploration of the topics to generate more definitive answers for the complex questions.

Reviewing Basic Legal Issues

Individuals involved in school-to-work endeavors are subject to a number of laws that impact such activities. The primary laws of concern are the Fair Labor Standards Act, the Federal Wage and Hour Act, and child labor laws. According to *School-to-Work Opportunities and the Fair Labor Standards Act: A Guide to Work-Based Learning, Federal Child Labor Laws, and Minimum Wage Provisions* (Office of School-to-Work Opportunities, 1995), School-to-Work activities involve learning experiences that equip participants for effective practice in the world of work. Nevertheless, not all learning experiences involve the concept of employment. Activities occurring in the workplace that do not involve the performance of work are not considered employment subject to the Fair Labor Standards Act (FLSA). Examples of these activities are field trips to a work site, job shadowing, and career awareness and exploration.

When is a learning experience, even though it might involve the performance of work, not considered employment? According to *School-to-Work Opportunities and the Fair Labor Standards Act* (Office of School-to-Work Opportunities, 1995), a student enrolled in a school-to-work learning experience would not be considered an employee within the meaning of the FLSA if all of the following criteria are met:

1. The student receives ongoing instruction at the employer's work site, as well as close on-site supervision throughout the learning experience, with the result that any productive work that the student performs is offset by the burden to the employer for the training and supervision provided.
2. The placement of the student at a work site during the learning experience does not result in the displacement of any regular employee; in other words, the presence of the student at the work site cannot result in an employee's being laid off, cannot result in the employer's not hiring an employee it would otherwise hire, and cannot result in an employee's working fewer hours than he or she would otherwise work.
3. The student is not entitled to a job at the completion of the learning experience, but this does not mean that employers are to be discouraged from offering employment to students who successfully complete the training.
4. The employer, student, and parent or guardian understand that the student is not entitled to wages or other compensation for the time spent in the learning experience, although the student may be paid a stipend for expenses such as books or tools.

In addition, the "level of performance" at which the student works or whether the work is of some educational or therapeutic benefit is immaterial. For purposes of the FLSA, the definition of *employ* is "to suffer or permit one to work" (Office of School-to-Work Opportunities, 1995, p. 5). Consequently, one might be working at a very low level in an organization or deriving some educational benefit from the "employment experience," but the experience would still be subject to the jurisdiction of the FLSA. It must be pointed out, however, that employment is defined differently under different laws, such as those dealing with income tax, workers' compensation, occupational safety and health, unemployment insurance, and others.

If the standards for employment are met and the enterprise or the student is covered under the FLSA, the student must be paid no less than the minimum wage, receive no less than one and one-half times the regular rate of pay for each hour worked in excess of forty per work week, and be employed in accordance with child labor laws. Even if the standards for employment are not met, payment of a stipend can be made; however, it cannot be used as a substitute for wages. A stipend is generally limited to reimbursement for expenses such as books, tuition, or tools. While child labor laws do not apply if there is not an employment relationship, school-to-work systems are encouraged to adhere to child labor laws with regard to hazardous working conditions.

Instruction and training in occupations that involve cutting or slicing machinery are obviously dangerous to children, and children should not be subjected to such machinery (Office of School-to-Work Opportunities, 1995). Additional information concerning this subject may be found in the National Institute for Occupational Safety and Health (1995) publication *Request for Assistance in Preventing Deaths and Injuries of Adolescent Workers*.

When are student employee situations covered by the FLSA? The act covers employees who are performing work for any type of enterprise that is either engaged in interstate commerce, producing goods for interstate commerce, or handling, selling, or otherwise working on goods or materials that have been moved or produced for such commerce. The FLSA covers enterprises

1. With annual gross volume of sales or business of not less than $500,000
2. Engaged in the operation of a hospital, an institution primarily engaged in the care of those who are physically or mentally ill or disabled or aged and who reside on the premises, a school for children who are mentally or physically disabled or gifted, a preschool, an elementary or secondary school, or an institution of higher education (whether operated for profit or not for profit)
3. That are activities of a public agency (Office of School-to-Work Opportunities, 1995)

Even if a student works for an enterprise that is not covered by the FLSA, the student may still be covered, depending upon the nature of the work he or she performs. For example, if the student takes or places out-of-state phone calls for a business, he or she would still be covered by the FLSA, even if the enterprise were not covered.

There are, however, exceptions to the FLSA standard for student learners and apprentices. A "student learner" is one who is enrolled in a course of study and training in a cooperative vocational training program under a recognized state or local educational authority or in a course of study in a substantially similar program conducted by a private school. An apprentice is a participant in an apprenticeship program legally registered by the Department of Labor's Bureau of Apprenticeship and Training or by an authorized state agency.

In addition, if a school or business holds a student subminimum wage certificate issued by a federal regional wage and hour division office, it may pay the following individuals a subminimum wage: students with disabilities participating in a school-related work program, student learners in a vocational education program, and full-time students in retail or service establishments, agriculture, or institutions of higher education.

Determining Standards and Limitations for Employment of Minors

Once it is determined that there is an employment relationship that is covered by the FLSA, then certain standards and limitations apply to the employment of students according to age. While there are no federal "hour limitations" on the number of hours a sixteen- seventeen-year-old youth may work in a non-farm job, or limitations on the time of day such work takes place, certain states do have such restrictions, and readers must be aware of the laws of their particular state. There are, however, limitations on the type of occupation in which a sixteen- or seventeen-year-old may work.

Seventeen nonfarm occupations are considered too hazardous for youths under the age of eighteen. Descriptions of those occupations are beyond the scope of this endeavor, and readers are advised to contact their regional office of the Wage and Hour Division of the Employment Standards Administration at the U.S. Department of Labor to obtain a list of the Hazardous Occupations Orders (HOs). It must also be pointed out that, under specified conditions, seven occupations listed under the HOs permit the use of sixteen- and seventeen-year-old youths as apprentices and student learners. Once again, Department of Labor guidelines are available to assist in such special situations.

Youths aged fourteen and fifteen also may be employed in nonfarm occupations predicated upon certain hours worked and occupational limitations. *School-to-Work Opportunities and the Fair Labor Standards Act* (Office of School-to-Work Opportunities, 1995) indicates that a fourteen- or fifteen-year-old may be utilized, but such work is limited to outside school hours, no more than three hours on a school day, no more than eighteen hours in a school week, no more than eight hours on a nonschool day, and no more than forty hours in nonschool weeks; furthermore, work must be performed only between 7 a.m. and 7 p.m. (although between June 1 and Labor Day, students may work as late as 9 p.m.).

The same occupational limitations as mentioned previously apply to this age group, and there are additional ones as well. There are no exceptions to occupational limitations such as those mentioned previously for student learners and apprentices.

Students under the age of fourteen may participate in school-to-work education and training activities, but employment may not be a component of the program. Activities may include, but are not limited to, presentations in the classroom by employers and employees, field trips to businesses, and job shadowing (whereby a student follows and observes an employee in his or her activities but performs no work).

Aligning Agricultural Activities and School-to-Work Programs

Youths under the age of sixteen enrolled in school-to-work activities may be employed in farm jobs, but the child labor regulations contain limitations on their employment and generally limit work to periods outside local public school hours. Students aged sixteen and older may be employed in any farm job at any time. Additional information concerning the employment of minors in agriculture may be found by referring to the *Child Labor Requirements in Agriculture under the Fair Labor Standards Act* (U.S. Department of Labor, 1995).

Verifying Worker Age

The FLSA requires employers to keep on file the date of birth of every employee under the age of nineteen. Because youths under the age of nineteen might be motivated to misstate their age in order to obtain employment and cause employers to unwittingly violate the minimum age standards of the act, employers are strongly advised to obtain an official age certificate that proves the validity of the date of birth.

Relating Federal Law to State and Local Laws

Whenever there are differences between federal standards and state and local standards, the stricter standard applies. For example, if a state has no minimum wage law, the federal minimum wage applies. If a state has a minimum wage higher than the federal minimum wage, the state standard applies.

Obtaining Waivers of the FLSA or Other Federal Regulations

The law specifically prohibits the waiver of any statutory or regulatory requirements under any provision relating to labor standards and occupational safety and health. Section 6212 of the School-to-Work Opportunities Act of 1994 also specifically prohibits such waivers. If a situation involves an employment relationship and the work is covered by FLSA, the employer must meet all statutory and regulatory requirements for the employment of minors.

Protecting School-to-Work Participants

According to McCord (1992), since systems and employers are not allowed any waivers regarding public health or safety, occupational safety and health, or environmental protection, employers and systems are strongly advised to be cognizant of basic public policies underlying tort law, which include those concerning fairness (those who cause harm should bear its costs), compensation (an injured party should have access to remedy for an injury inflicted by another), and prevention (holding an individual responsible for his or her wrongs). Appropriate liability insurance is a "must" for school-to-work programs.

Establishing Standards for Accountability and Quality

Even though there are legal requirements that both educational systems and employers must meet in a school-to-work program, it must be stressed that the educational system must maintain control of standards for program or academic accountability. Educators should have the final determination, based upon input from the field, relative to program quality.

Resolving Technological Issues

Technology is effectively eliminating the traditional boundaries of education and becoming a tool whereby anyone can learn anywhere, anytime, and at any age. The last time our world witnessed such incredible changes in technology was during what is now called the Industrial Revolution. As the result of that era, many people relocated to cities to work with others. Today, however, distance is becoming unimportant because of the proliferation of new technologies. A trained and knowledgeable workforce is one of the major keys to economic success for individuals, businesses, and our nation, and with the emergence of the technology age and the global economy, learners must be able to compete with the worldwide workforce.

Technological changes are occurring so rapidly that it is difficult for educators to remain updated, and educators must be aware of how these changes will impact service-area designations and instructional practices. Technological advances are forcing employees to engage in continuous learning, critical thinking, and teamwork.

Establishing the Technology Infrastructure

The Commission for a Competitive North Carolina (1995, p. 27) identified the challenge of providing an infrastructure for ever-changing and ever-expanding technology that includes

- Increasing technological advances and contributions to the knowledge base generated within the state
- Ensuring that advanced telecommunications are accessible and affordable

- Encouraging the diffusion of technology to business and people
- Providing dedicated funds to finance infrastructure needs

The Governor's Commission on Workforce Preparedness (1995) reported that a workforce development system cannot succeed without a sound infrastructure. Key characteristics of workforce development must include the integrated delivery of service and the electronic sharing of information across providers. Agencies to be involved include community colleges, public schools, employment security commissions, those connected with the Job Training Partnership Act, or with vocational rehabilitation and social services. These agencies must be aware that the technological changes require the infrastructure necessary to support the technology.

The Association of Community College Trustees also is acutely aware of the fundamental changes that technology is forcing upon community colleges. As reported by Warren (1995), Don Doucette, vice chancellor for educational services and instructional technology for the Metropolitan Community Colleges of Kansas City, Missouri, emphasized that our nation is on the verge of a crisis in higher education. Community colleges need to reinvent themselves in order to respond to the challenges presented by technology. Doucette also argues that the college of the future will be built on an infrastructure not made of bricks and mortar, but of networks. It was his feeling that neither the young student of today nor the adult working student will be satisfied with sitting through a traditional fifty-minute college lecture.

Posing Solutions

What can be done to keep up with such an ever-changing resource? Experts advise that colleges must develop a technology plan as a part of their long-range plans. Planners can no longer hope for a one-time grant to try a new technology but must budget for continued demands to keep up with technological changes. Institutional technological policies must be developed that address adherence to software licenses, appropriate usage, intellectual property rights, and guidelines for Web servers and those accessing the Internet.

Bringing the issue into focus on workforce development, educators must be conscious that learning has shifted from teacher-centered learning to learner-centered learning. Students being trained through workforce development programs must be trained on equipment that has progressed along with the technological changes.

The question is, how do educators plan the technology infrastructure to enhance reformation and restructuring of learning within our institutions? What steps must be taken to develop the training necessary to acquaint teachers with on-line databases on the Internet, establish electronic communication between educational institutions and the rest of the world, and develop distance learning opportunities between educational institutions and industry? Are apprenticeships the answer for student exposure to current technological advances in the workplace?

These questions must be addressed, and financial resources must be allocated so that community colleges are not left behind in global technological advances. The business world is shouting for a more knowledgeable and skilled workforce. This can be accomplished by focusing on school-to-work programs, recognizing the ability of our students to learn, and providing the technology necessary to train them.

Assessing Additional Help

The purpose of this chapter is to provide accurate and authoritative information of a general character only. Neither the authors nor the publisher is engaged in rendering legal advice. Readers are strongly advised to contact a regional office of the Wage and Hour Division of the Employment Standards Administration of the U.S. Department of Labor or their attorney for specific advice regarding particular issues involving the School-to-Work Opportunities Act.

References

Commission for a Competitive North Carolina. *Measuring Up to the Challenge: A Prosperous North Carolina in a Competitive World.* Raleigh, N.C.: Commission for a Competitive North Carolina, May 1995.

Governor's Commission on Workforce Preparedness. *Building a High-Performance Workforce: 1995–97 Strategic Directions for North Carolina, Executive Summary.* Raleigh, N.C.: Governor's Commission on Workforce Preparedness, 1995.

Laanan, F. S. "Community Colleges as Facilitators of School-to-Work." *ERIC Digest.* Los Angeles: ERIC Clearinghouse for Community Colleges, 1995. (ED 383 360)

McCord, J. *Litigation Paralegal: A Systems Approach.* (2nd ed.) St. Paul, Minn.: West Publishing, 1992.

National Institute for Occupational Safety and Health. *Request for Assistance in Preventing Deaths and Injuries of Adolescent Workers* (DHHS Publication No. 95–125). Cincinnati, Ohio: U.S. Department of Health and Human Services, Public Health Service, Centers for Disease Control and Prevention, National Institute for Occupational Safety and Health, 1995.

Office of School-to-Work Opportunities, U.S. Departments of Education and Labor. *School-to-Work Opportunities and the Fair Labor Standards Act: A Guide to Work-Based Learning, Federal Child Labor Laws, and Minimum Wage Provisions.* Washington, D.C.: National School-to Work Office, 1995.

U.S. Department of Labor, Wage and Hour Division of the Employment Standards Administration. *The Child Labor Requirements in Agriculture Under the Fair Labor Standards Act* (Child Labor Bulletin No. 102). Washington, D.C.: U.S. Government Printing Office, 1995.

Warren, A. "Technology Forcing Fundamental Change in Two-Year Colleges." *Association of Community College Trustees Advisor,* 1995, 25(6), 8–9.

DONALD W. BRYANT *is president of Carteret Community College, Morehead City, North Carolina.*

MARY P. KIRK *is assistant to the president at Carteret Community College, Morehead City, North Carolina.*

The authors discuss how to achieve the school-to-work goal of having a systemic effect. The chapter provides practical examples from prior workforce education innovations and touches on the financial implications of implementing school-to-work programs in community colleges.

School-to-Work Systems and the Community College: Looking Ahead

Edgar I. Farmer, Cassy B. Key

Community colleges have been a vital force in ferreting out, responding to, and serving the diverse needs of those in their service areas. Community colleges bridge urban and rural interests; link secondary education, apprenticeship training, and four-year colleges; provide remediation; and upgrade the technical skills of incumbent workers so they can stay abreast of an increasingly technology-centered workplace (Baker, 1994). Through a smorgasbord of associate degree, registered apprenticeship, certificate, adult basic, and continuing education programs, community colleges have traditionally improved the general public's quality of life (Boone, 1992). Today, community colleges have added the role of drawing together diverse constituencies in their service regions—while continuing to provide high-quality education and training at the most reasonable costs (Roueche, Taber, and Roueche, 1995).

As an extension of their traditions, community colleges have the power and ethical responsibility to negotiate systemic education reform, first suggested in the 1970s career education movement, in the Tech-Prep Act of 1990, and later in the School-to-Work Opportunities Act of 1994 (STWOA). Experts predict that 65 percent of future jobs will require education beyond high school but not a four-year college degree (Gray and Herr, 1995). By responding to the new workforce education market, community colleges can prepare most American workers—both those in the workplace today and those just entering—for successful employment. Assuming this role, however, will require effort and proactive commitment to collaboration and partnerships with educators, labor, and employers.

Analyzing Today's Workforce Education Environment

Employers are still spending or losing $60 billion per year on illiterate work-ers (Gerstner, 1994). At the same time, Hedrick Smith (1995) wonders "how long rank-and-file workers who are falling behind economically will continue to tolerate growing disparities in earnings without social protest." He cites then Labor Secretary Robert Reich's reference to the new "anxious class" of Ameri-cans (p. 412), for whom job security is an anachronism. The recent Roueche, Taber, and Roueche (1995) study suggests there is much pressure from legis-lators, boards, and faculty to limit community colleges to traditional school-ing—to do less with less. Some would limit the community college role to simply providing a core of instruction in academic and technical subjects, with less emphasis on the role of community service.

Recent welfare reform, "one-stop career shops" (career centers), and "work-first" initiatives offer potential to community colleges as service providers. These reforms also will make the outcomes of community colleges more visi-ble and may put community college training in competition with education and training offered by entrepreneurs and competitive institutions. Market conditions have changed.

Technical training in community colleges has been the poor cousin of lib-eral arts transfer programs, forced to operate with outdated faculty and anti-quated equipment. In an era of declining federal funding, some believe that school-to-work and other federal workforce education funds should be tar-geted to second-chance, rather than first-chance programs, and only to areas where the need is greatest. The issue of spending federal funds for second-chance versus first-chance programs can become a political football. For exam-ple, 33 percent of the students enrolled in community colleges already hold baccalaureate degrees, and they are returning to postsecondary two-year insti-tutions to acquire the skills necessary to compete in the workforce (Gray and Herr, 1995).

As these political forces evolve, traditional instruction—or business as usual in the "ivory tower" academic-transfer community college—will not be enough to position community colleges as full players in the new workforce education market. In short, community colleges will either lead or be pushed out of the way as preferred training providers for technical workers—the result of a combination of factors, including tightening funding streams, the need for updated technology, antiquated attitudes among faculty, increased accountabil-ity, more sophisticated industry training programs, increased privatization, and politicization. Boone's 1992 study, however, cites four major strengths of the nation's network of community colleges that can help them assume the leader-ship-catalyst role in their respective communities. First, community colleges, uniquely American and democratic from their inception, are deeply embedded in the fabric of their communities, fueled for the most part by local taxes. They are inextricably linked by virtue of their mission and record of achievements to economic development. Second, most community colleges have a multidisciplinary and comprehensive focus unequaled by other community-based or proprietary organizations. Third, community colleges are seen as the "user-friendly" approach to higher education, the site of many first-generation college students' entrance into technical ("gold-collar") jobs and professional careers. And fourth, community colleges are viewed as neutral organizations committed to serving all the people. As education becomes further politicized, the ability to be a neutral convener is important. Community college leadership is usually sensitive to the social, economic, and political forces that shape the community environment. However, the new market will be won by those who choose their partners wisely.

Concerns Sparking the Development of the STWOA

Several concerns sparked the development of the STWOA: the need for better training for students not attending a four-year institution, increased global economic competitiveness and a changing workplace, an undersupply of technically prepared workers, and research from cognitive psychologists such as Resnick (1987) and Berryman (Berryman and Bailey, 1992) and others such as Grubb (Grubb and others, 1991) suggesting that students achieve higher academic and occupational standards when they learn in context rather than in the abstract.

The work-based learning approach, modeled after the time-honored apprenticeship concept, integrates theoretical instruction with structured on-the-job training. This approach, combined with school-based learning, can be effective in engaging student interest among both the college-bound (Hamilton, 1990) and non-college-bound, enhancing skill acquisition, developing positive work attitudes, and preparing youth for high-skill, high-wage careers (Grubb and others, 1991). In addition, in 1992 approximately 3,400,000 U.S. youth aged sixteen to twenty-four had not completed high school and were not enrolled in school—a number representing about 11 percent of all those in this age group—indicating that these members of the potential labor pool were particularly unprepared for the demands of a twenty-first century workplace (Imel, 1995; School-to-Work Opportunities Act of 1994).

Outlining the Innovations in the STWOA

The purposes of the STWOA are numerous. Its strengths are in its emphasis on utilizing workplaces as active learning parts of the educational process by making employers joint partners with educators and promoting the formation of local partnerships dedicated to linking the worlds of school and work among secondary and postsecondary institutions, private and public employers, labor organizations, government, community-based organizations, parents, students, state educational agencies, local educational agencies, and training and human service agencies.

These partnerships are encouraged to build on a range of promising school-to-work activities, such as tech-prep education plans, career academies, school-to-apprenticeship programs, cooperative education, youth apprenticeships, school-based enterprises, business-education compacts, and promising strategies that assist school dropouts.

School-to-work programs require high-quality, paid work-based learning experiences. The goal is to expose students to a broad array of career opportunities and to facilitate the selection of career majors based on individual students' interests, goals, strengths, and abilities.

Signed into law on the south lawn of the White House on May 4, 1994, as Public Law 103-239, the STWOA represented, as President Bill Clinton stated, a new approach to work and learning. David Pierce (1994), president of the American Association of Community Colleges, agreed with Clinton, asserting that community colleges would have a central role in the Clinton initiative. A postsecondary element in the STWOA recognized both the higher liberal arts and technical skill levels and the lifelong learning needs of youth wishing to compete effectively in a high-wage economy.

Administering the STWOA

The STWOA was defined by Halperin (1994) as a broad, community-based effort to prepare all young people for success both academically and professionally. It specifies three major components: school-based learning, focusing on both industry settings and classroom instruction and high academic and vocational skill standards; work-site learning, focusing on work experiences, structured training, and mentoring in the workplace; and connecting activities, focusing on courses and activities, consortia creation and leadership, and programs that integrate classroom and on-the-job instruction.

Illuminating the Three Components of the STWOA

The STWOA is identical to the education plans in the Tech-Prep Act that preceded it, with one exception. In addition to integrated curricula developed jointly by employers, labor, and educators; a comprehensive career development system; and the selection of a major, the STWOA requires a work-based component. During a 1996 international study tour sponsored by the W. K. Kellogg Foundation through North Carolina State University, participants were surprised to find Western European employers and union stewards in Germany, Great Britain, Belgium, and France complaining in unison about the dollars and length of time the apprenticeship system is taking. Those interviewed at job centers, career centers, chambers of commerce, universities, and the European Commission observed that employers often say they want the impossible—outstanding high school graduates with great skills, a master's degree, and fluency in three languages.

Perhaps tech-prep programs, the cornerstone of the STWOA and an American invention, require another American invention—the community college—as a connection. That connection can facilitate one cost-effective way of improving the labor force while shortening the education process.

School-based learning in community colleges should include academic work in the student's career major and at least one year of postsecondary education leading to a skill certificate. According to the law, tech-prep programs are an example of school-based learning activities; however, how they should be implemented continues to be debated.

Bragg's 1995 research suggests that in implementation practice, tech-prep programs combine academic and occupation-oriented education and use applied academics or other approaches to curriculum integration. They also require formal articulation between secondary and postsecondary institutions, ensuring that the last two years of high school are connected by curriculum plans to two years of college, leading to an associate degree.

Key (1994) first suggested that successful tech-prep implementation would require more than attention to curricular issues, advocating that tech-prep "systems" should be housed in consortia of sufficient magnitude to create a critical mass (to ensure systemic reform) and that the scope of work should include comprehensive counseling, professional development, participative planning, and information dissemination to all stakeholders; the inclusion of related liberal arts studies and work-based learning; 4 + 2 + 2 or beyond articulation of curricula; the integration of academic-technical and postsecondary-secondary-industry curricular models and strategies; and evaluation that pays increasing attention to authentic assessment. Key (1991) also asserted that, if implemented with attention to these systemic details, tech-prep initiatives could maximize the education reform process while leveraging human and financial resources.

Key (1991, 1994) also saw large-scale tech-prep consortia, later implemented statewide across Texas (providing access for all students), as vehicles for engaging employers and labor, bringing better focus to student outcomes, updating curricula, enhancing student employability, improving institutional effectiveness, and creating communication lines across communities and regions, thereby enhancing regional economic-development practices.

Key's 1994 synthesis of research related to tech-prep outcomes concluded the following:

1. Tech-prep is not just a program or specific curriculum. It is a system of activities that has already produced successful students.
2. Tech-prep systems also can include an evaluation component that links each academic program to business, industry, and labor and leads to ongoing refinement.
3. Tech-prep programs' rigorous and holistic approach to creating a better qualified workforce can link the strengths of the vocational-technical high school–community college–technical school domain to the liberal arts domain.

Key's 1994 study also suggested that the Tech-Prep Act's strength, like that of the STWOA, is in offering students various incentives, such as assessment, career awareness activities, and counseling, including the accommodation of the needs of special populations; the chance to take and succeed in college courses—often for free—while still in high school; and an opportunity for smoother school-to-work transition (if the education plan includes work-based learning). Since tech-prep programs are linked to high-priority job opportunities in the act (a deviation from the STWOA), tech-prep career majors retain the option of higher degrees. If the STWOA is to succeed, it will need to build on the experiences of the Tech-Prep Act and similar initiatives, not reinvent them. Tech-prep programs have been incorporating many of the same criteria as those suggested in the STWOA, including the use of registered apprenticeships, curriculum development and integration, career development, and work-based learning.

Bragg's 1995 study advocated six core concepts tech-prep programs need in order to become educational reform mechanisms. First, tech-prep education plans must be grounded in an integrated and authentic (that is, real-world or simulation of real-world) core curriculum at both the secondary and postsecondary levels. Second, a fully integrated and authentic 2 + 2 core curriculum leads to the second fundamental component of tech-prep programs—formal articulation. Third, rather than perpetuate current practices, tech-prep programs should build bridges to connect the theory and practice inherent in both academic and vocational education—an idea advocated nearly a century ago by John Dewey (1915). Fourth, Bragg suggests that practitioners develop an outcomes-focused curriculum to firmly establish the tech-prep concept as a standards-driven, performance-based educational initiative. Fifth, tech-prep programs should address the needs of all students, including those at the top and bottom 25 percent (the "all-students" concept so well defined in the STWOA). Bragg's sixth concept promotes collaborative implementation to ensure that the other five components operate effectively together.

Work-site learning includes instructional programs focused on work experiences, structured training, and mentoring in the workplace. This aspect of the school-to-work education plan requires labor and business partners willing to give education more than lip service—partners willing to roll up their sleeves and participate in the sometimes grueling practice of teaching and mentoring. Here again, school-to-work programs should build on related current practices. For example, Junior Achievement curriculum teaches middle school students to build and then dismantle businesses. Junior Achievement is also on the forefront of the school-to-work movement. Although implementing Junior Achievement requires financial contributions from the community's business community, this model successfully transmits the American notions of entrepreneurship and the free enterprise system. Therefore, Junior Achievement is a logical member of the community-based organizations with a stake in the STWOA. Junior Achievement is available only to secondary schools, however.

What about the quality of work sites? Of mentors? Legal issues involving underaged youth? In an occupation as volatile as electronics—or among small, niche-marketed, entrepreneurial high-tech companies—sustaining the participation of masses of youth through paid internships may be difficult. Middle- and small-sized companies, which form the bulk of our economy, seldom can afford their own training programs; many rely on community colleges for this service. Perhaps, however, a wide-reaching media campaign or statewide job development plan can reach the large number of employers and labor organizations necessary to sustain the massive work-based learning needed for both secondary and postsecondary school-to-work students.

The late director of the National Center for Research in Vocational Education at the University of California, Berkeley, Charles Benson, was a strong advocate for the STWOA. He had one overriding concern, however: "Where are the jobs?" (personal communication, 1993). The current director, David Stern (Stern and others, 1994), helped address that concern in his enthusiasm for something old with a new twist: school-based enterprise. According to Stern and his fellow researchers, "Every year, tens of thousands of high school students across the country participate in school-based enterprises . . . build houses, publish books, run restaurants, produce original scientific research, staff child-care centers, and provide other goods and services. . . . Productive activities can also help students learn academic subjects and develop general intellectual abilities" (book jacket). According to a 1992 national survey of public secondary schools, 18.6 percent were sponsoring at least one school-based enterprise (Stern, 1992). Community colleges would do well to investigate the potential of school-based enterprises, drawing on the resources of businesses built by students that add financial resources to college coffers and often add jobs to communities, particularly in inner-city urban and isolated rural areas.

Another useful vehicle: the REAL (Rural Entrepreneurship through Action Learning) curriculum. The REAL program, a promising venture that originated in Georgia, is designed to teach entrepreneurship skills from kindergarten through college. Jonathan Sher (1977) had the notion of community development corporations linked to schools; he joined forces with Paul Allergy to create REAL. REAL is used more in community colleges than in secondary schools. The creation of REAL enterprises allows students to build and succeed in businesses. Since community colleges often are a community's small-business incubator, there might be a natural transition of that work to classrooms.

In short, becoming a "learning organization" (Senge, 1990) may well include becoming an "earning" organization as well. Implementing work-based learning on a large scale in community college programs will mean that substantial extra dollars may be needed, especially at community colleges where cooperative (co-op) education is not standard practice.

Systemic reform related to school-to-work programs has already begun. In Texas, work-based learning has been mandated as part of all technical programs in community and technical colleges by September 1997. That decision has financial implications. It means adding faculty capable of solidifying relationships with business and labor partners and monitoring the effectiveness of work-based learning, adding staff who can find out where students are working and use those contacts to start partnerships, adding data processing staff who can monitor the success of graduates beyond their first job, educating faculty about the advisability of employing new teaching strategies, connecting each education plan to work-based learning opportunities, adding administrative staff to assist in curriculum development and revision in order to update degree plans, and perhaps offering job placement services as a perk for students and graduates (Dale Gares, personal communication, 1996).

If block-grant funding removes workforce education funding from the locally elected school boards and puts allocation decisions under the supervision of local workforce development boards, long-range planning for programs and resources will force community colleges to become both more collaborative and more entrepreneurial. Indeed, both school-based enterprises and public-private partnerships offer much promise in filling instructional and financial gaps in the future. Implementing STWOA reform in community colleges will call for stepping out onto an unknown path—to take what Hedrick Smith refers to as "the Japanese path to ultimate success . . . *kaizen,* the incremental accumulation of skill and know-how, continuous improvement" (1995, p. 8). In short, the work-based learning and connecting activities components of the STWOA will require community colleges to rethink who they do business with and the way they do business. This will include facility use, admissions, class scheduling, the definition of excellence in instruction, the credentialing and grading process, faculty evaluation, and the delivery and kinds of professional development deemed necessary for institutional effectiveness. Institutions that rethink early on and become what Senge calls learning organizations will succeed well into the twenty-first century; others may not.

Connecting activities are designed to ease the transition from in-school to out-of-school learning in the workplace (Bragg, 1995). In other words, activities that connect school and work should coordinate classroom instruction and workplace experiences so that the school-based instructional program reinforces what is taught at the work site and matches students (presumably also graduates) with employers. Examples of connecting activities in community colleges may be career counseling, job placement, workplace mentoring, technical assistance, staff development, and other support services. In any event, much of what occurs under the STWOA's work-based learning component requires a connecting activity: providing site mentors and liaisons between schools and employers, providing professional development and technical assistance to employers about to become mentors, providing job developers to locate learning sites, linking participants to social and community services, and conducting evaluation of program outcomes.

Most youths and their parents understand that college is the path to a preferred future; however, only about 25 percent graduate, leaving the rest adrift, getting a message that society has little more for them than a minimum-wage job (Resnick and Wirt, 1996). The STWOA advocates decreasing the "drift factor" to provide a smoother transition into the workforce. Resnick and Wirt (1996) assert that a shift to education that is standards-driven and governed by outputs, with rewards closely tied to performance and effort, makes more sense. With the attention being given to local control, national curriculum standards, for example, would ensure consistent quality.

To be truly effective, however, the STWOA's interpretation of connecting activities should be broad, including the development of regional consortia or the inclusion of third-party intermediaries so that shared vision among communities can occur. Although this means sharing the power, the potential trade-off is impressive. For example, according to Dale Gares, associate vice president of Austin Community College, there is enormous financial potential for community colleges in these connections. Through Austin Community College's partnership with the Capital Area Training Foundation, an employer-led intermediary organization, the college has been able to add almost $1 million to the development of a semiconductor program (D. Gares, personal communication, 1996). However, without creating a network of sufficient size to create knowledge and to create the necessary critical mass for broad-scale implementation, the STWOA will not succeed. Just working harder individually will not be working smart.

By their traditions, community colleges are well suited to connect their communities to the future. The authors believe that the enlightened self-interest of community colleges will compel them to take an active role in implementing the STWOA and that this sourcebook will help support those activities. For as Margaret Wheatley (1992) points out, "It is information that gives order, that prompts growth, that defines what is alive. It is both the underlying structure and the dynamic process that ensures life" (p. 102).

References

Baker, G. A. *Handbook on the Community College in America: Its History, Mission, and Management.* Westport, Conn.: Greenwood Press, 1994.

Berryman, S. E., and Bailey, T. *The Double Helix: Education and the Economy.* New York: Teachers College Press, 1992.

Boone, E. *Community-Based Programming: An Opportunity and Imperative for the Community College.* Raleigh: Department of Adult and Community College Education, North Carolina State University, 1992.

Bragg, D. "Linking High Schools to Postsecondary Institutions: The Role of Tech Prep." In W. N. Grubb (ed.), *Education Through Occupations in American High Schools: The Challenges of Implementing Curriculum Integration.* 2 vols. New York: Columbia University, Teachers College, 1995.

Dewey, J. *The School and Society.* (rev. ed.) Chicago: University of Chicago Press, 1915.

Gerstner, L. "Our Schools Are Failing. Do We Care?" *New York Times,* May 27, 1994, p. A27.

Gray, K. C., and Herr, E. L. *Other Ways to Win: Creating Alternatives for High School Graduates.* Thousand Oaks, Calif.: Corwin Press, 1995.

Grubb, W. N., and others. *The Cunning Hand, the Cultured Mind: Models for Integrating Vocational and Academic Education.* Berkeley: National Center for Research in Vocational Education, University of California, Berkeley, 1991.

Halperin, S. *School-to-Work: A Larger Vision*. Washington, D.C.: American Youth Policy Forum, 1994.

Hamilton, S. F. *Apprenticeship for Adulthood: Preparing Youth for the Future*. New York: Free Press, 1990.

Imel, S. *School-to-Work Transition, Trends and Issues* (ERIC Alerts, ERIC Clearinghouse on Adult, Career, and Vocational Education). Columbus, Ohio: Center on Education and Training for Employment, Ohio State University, 1995.

Key, C. "Building Tech-Prep Systems Geared for the Twenty-First Century." Unpublished doctoral dissertation, University of Texas, Austin, 1991.

Key, C. "Synthesis of Literature Related to Tech-Prep Outcomes." In G. Baker (ed.), *A Handbook on the Community College in America*. Westport, Conn.: Greenwood Press, 1994.

Pierce, D. School-to-work letter to members of the association. Unpublished documents. Washington, D.C.: American Association of Community Colleges, 1994.

Resnick, L. B. *Education and Learning to Think*. Washington, D.C.: National Academy Press, 1987.

Resnick, L. B., and Wirt, J. (eds.). *Linking School and Work: Roles for Standards and Assessment*. San Francisco: Jossey-Bass, 1996.

Roueche, J., Taber, L., and Roueche, S. *The Company We Keep: Collaboration in the Community College*. Washington, D.C.: Community College Press, 1995.

Senge, P. *The Fifth Discipline: The Art and Practice of the Learning Organization*. New York: Doubleday, 1990.

Sher, J. P. (ed.). *Education in Rural America: A Reassessment of Conventional Wisdom*. Boulder, Colo.: Westview Press, 1977.

Smith, H. *Rethinking America: Innovative Strategies and Partnerships in Business and Education*. New York: Random House, 1995.

Stern, D. *School-to-Work Programs and Services in Secondary Schools and Two-Year Public Postsecondary Institutions: Findings from the National Assessment of Vocational Education Survey*. Berkeley: School of Education, University of California, 1992.

Stern, D., Stone, J., III, Hopkins, C., McMillion, M., and Crain, R. *School-Based Enterprise: Productive Learning in American High Schools*. San Francisco: Jossey-Bass, 1994.

Wheatley, M. J. *Leadership and the New Science: Learning About Organization from an Orderly Universe*. San Francisco: Berrett-Koehler, 1992.

Edgar I. Farmer *is associate professor of workforce education and development at Pennsylvania State University.*

Cassy B. Key *is executive director of the Capital Area Tech-Prep/School-to-Work Consortium in Austin, Texas.*

This article provides an annotated bibliography of materials from the ERIC system highlighting the role of community colleges in school-to-work initiatives.

Sources and Information: School-to-Work Programming and Initiatives in the United States

Matthew Burstein

American community colleges, with their overt mission of meeting the educational and training needs of the local community, are uniquely positioned to assist in school-to-work (STW) programs. By modifying their current relationships to secondary schools and local business and industry, community colleges can facilitate STW efforts, including tech-prep initiatives.

The following publications reflect the current ERIC literature on transfer programs and articulation agreements. Most ERIC documents (publications with ED numbers) can be viewed on microfiche at over nine hundred libraries worldwide. In addition, most may be ordered on microfiche or on paper from the ERIC Document Reproduction Service (EDRS) by calling (800) 443-ERIC. Journal articles are not available from EDRS, but they can be acquired through regular library channels or purchased from the University Microfilm International Articles Clearinghouse, which can be reached at (800) 248–0360.

School-to-Work: General Information

The articles in this section provide general information about STW programs.

Batt, R., and Osterman, P. *A National Policy for Workplace Training. Lessons from State and Local Experiments.* Washington, D.C.: Economic Policy Institute, 1993. (ED 373 140).

    Selected state and local experiments in developing and supporting workplace-centered training programs were analyzed to identify issues relevant to developing a national policy for workplace training. Case studies were conducted for the state economic development and training programs in California and Illinois and the employment and training programs provided by North and South Carolina's community college systems, and various joint training efforts involving unions, employers, local governments, and community organizations were reviewed. It was concluded that the federal government should fund a national training effort aimed at enhancing the skills of incumbent workers, states should be responsible for choosing the most effective means of administering federal training programs, and national training policy should focus on underserved groups and programs contributing to the establishment of strong employment and training systems. The importance of developing and implementing youth apprenticeship or STW transition programs was emphasized. It was recommended that funding for a national training policy come from either general revenue or a dedicated payroll tax. The start-up funding required for a national training policy was estimated at $375 million, with subsequent funding levels of $2 billion annually thereafter. The piece is 71 pages long, features an appendix with a table summarizing ten studies of the effects of skills and training on economic performance, and contains forty-nine references.

Glover, R. W., and others. *School-to-Work Transition in the U.S.: The Case of the Missing Social Partners. A Report of the Governance and Finance Team of the Comparative Learning Teams Project.* College Park, Md.: Center for Learning and Competitiveness, School of Public Affairs, University of Maryland, 1994. (ED 374 352)

A team of U.S. business, labor, and public policy representatives visited Denmark, Germany, and Switzerland to investigate the European approach to preparing young people for the workforce. It gathered information on the performance of governance and finance systems abroad and identified their key underlying principles and operations. Six common features were identified across the three countries, offering a sharp contrast to existing U.S. policies and practices: as a national policy, sixteen- to twenty-year-olds in Europe are engaged in mainstream workplaces as both workers and learners; vocational education is industry-driven through well-established systems; national frameworks developed through consensus of all partners provide strong direction to the vocational education system, without federal bureaucracy; initial training, further training, and retraining are becoming increasingly integrated; the investment in vocational training for youth among the partners is high; and views of accountability and responsibility prevail that contrast significantly with U.S. attitudes. The report is 40 pages long.

Pierce, D. "School-to-Work Transition Is Now Law." *AACC Letter* (Special Issue no. 1), 1994. (ED 370 631)

This special six-page edition of the *AACC Letter* is part of a continuing effort by the American Association of Community Colleges (AACC) to keep community colleges current with developments related to STW legislation. The newsletter begins with a summary of the AACC's efforts to influence bill language that would be favorable to community college participation in STW programs, a list of STW-related AACC professional development activities, and a statement encouraging state directors for community college education to become involved in the development of STW partnerships in their states. Included is an update on the present and future status of the STW implementation grant process.

School-to-Work Program Descriptions

These documents provide information about specific school-to-work initiatives on national, state, and local levels.

"Academic Program Articulation at Springfield Technical Community College: Building a Framework for Tech-Prep and School-to-Work." Materials presented at the Third Annual Conference on Workforce Training of the League for Innovation in the Community College, San Diego, California, February 8–11, 1995. (ED 379 039; for a related document, see JC 940 117)

Springfield Technical Community College was the first college in western Massachusetts to establish formal 2 + 2 articulation agreements with area high schools. As of September 1994 the college had signed a total of sixty-five individual agreements with nineteen schools relating to eighteen different associate degree programs. There are many benefits of curriculum articulation, but most importantly it produces more graduates with higher-level skills and clearer goals. The first phase of articulation includes exploration of possibilities with secondary schools, exchange of visits between institutions, development of recommended terms for an articulation, and approval and formal signing of the agreement. The second phase includes program promotion, student application for credit, and periodic agreement review. A typical articulation specifies the courses articulated and total number of credits awarded; a competency level for the awarding of credit; complementary course work that might be required; recommended courses for optimal preparation; each institution's commitment to some variety of promotional activity; encouragement of students to take college English and math placement tests in the spring of their senior year; an agreement to meet annually to review, refine, or expand the agreement; and recommendations reflecting particular interests or priorities in given fields (for example, invitations to various departmental or campus activities). Thirty-two pages; appendices include sample articulation agreements.

Evaluation and Training Institute. *School to Work Transition: Vocational Education Resource Package.* Los Angeles: Evaluation and Training Institute, 1993. (ED 357 794)

Designed to assist community college administrators and faculty in enhancing vocational education programs and services, this twenty-seven-page resource package provides information on school-to-work transition programs within the California Community Colleges (CCC). The opening section of the report discusses the changing demands of the job market and the impact on students' educational needs, describes demographic and economic trends likely to affect the job market and workforce by the year 2000, and reviews the foundation skills and competencies of effective workers, identified in the Secretary's Commission on Achieving Necessary Skills (SCANS) report for educational reform. The report describes two specific programs: Project Adelante at Long Beach City College, which provides vocational skills training, assistance, and guidance to disadvantaged, limited-English-proficient, and disabled vocational education students; and the Mathematics, Engineering, and Science Achievement Minority Engineering Program at Sacramento City College, which provides arenas for collaborative learning, personal and practical skills development, and a hands-on work experience program for minority students. The final section of the report draws from interviews of staff at CCC institutions and details strategies for successful school-to-work transition efforts, including gaining business and industry input in curriculum development, forming advisory committees, emphasizing cooperative work experience programs, forming long-range partnerships with primary and secondary schools, and implementing instruction that addresses personal qualities and job search skills.

Grubb, W. N., and Badway, N. *Linking School-Based and Work-Based Learning: The Implications of LaGuardia's Co-op Seminars for School-to-Work Programs.* Technical assistance report. Berkeley: National Center for Research in Vocational Education, University of California, Berkeley, 1995. (ED 388 861)

Co-op seminars are a key component of the cooperative education (CE) program at LaGuardia Community College in New York City. All LaGuardia students must enroll in CE and attend a series of co-op seminars that raise general issues about work, occupations in general, and the competencies required on the job. The seminars serve as a form of career exploration and a mechanism of connecting school- and work-based learning. Three levels of generic and major-specific seminars are offered. Like LaGuardia's CE program, the seminars attempt to promote an approach to teaching called TAR (Teach-Apply-Reinforce) and include classroom exercises and fieldwork assignments. Over the past decade, the co-op seminar program has undergone numerous changes, including a movement toward more generic seminars, greater flexibility, and use of union-sponsored and union-supported tutoring in basic skills. The co-op seminars incorporate a range of classroom techniques, including traditional lecture, class discussion, simulations and role playing, and faculty sharing of personal experiences. Thirty pages.

Illinois Community College Board. *The Illinois Community College System and the School-to-Work Transition Initiative: A Working Model.* Springfield: Illinois Community College Board, 1995. (ED 390 489)

Community colleges represent the ideal location for building the highly skilled workforce needed in a high tech society, since they are community-based and responsive to local needs. Through the school-to-work initiative of the Illinois Community College System (ICCS), colleges and secondary systems are working in partnership to promote successful transitions for students through technical, honors, and telecommunication programs. Currently, the ICCS serves nearly one million students annually, offering associate degree transfer programs, occupational degree and certificate programs, apprenticeship and work-based learning programs, bridge programs to prepare high school students with varying skill levels for college-level programs, youth-centered programs, and adult education. As part of its commitment to provide community services, the ICCS has developed a statewide telecommunications network designed to enhance educational opportunities for the community. It also provides business and industry training and retraining, career centers, small business development centers, technology centers, and manufacturing outreach centers. Twenty-eight pages.

Southern Maryland Educational Consortium. *Model Tech-Prep Demonstration Project. Final Report.* La Plata: Southern Maryland Educational Consortium, 1995. (ED 383 915)

The Southern Maryland Educational Consortium's Tech-Prep Model Demonstration project is described in this 211-page final report. The consortium members are the Calvert, Charles, and St. Mary's County school districts and Charles County Community College in southern Maryland. The project is based on a 4 + 2 model in which ninth-grade students develop career plans and follow career pathways in one of three technologies: health and human services, electronics and engineering, or business. The report highlights the activities of the two-year project grant period, including site visits, presentations by staff, preparation and distribution of tech-prep brochures, and participation in the European International Teleconference on Tech-Prep and School-to-Work. The appendices, which constitute more than 90 percent of this document, include the following: sample coordination team agendas; consortium objectives; lists of and information pertaining to site visits, national presentations, and technical assistance provided by project staff; project publicity materials; information about the independent firm hired to evaluate the project; project budget information, and a survey instrument. (For a final evaluation report, see CE 069 317.)

Wisconsin Technical College Systems Board. *The 1994–96 Two-Year Plan for the Use of Federal Funds Available Under the Carl D. Perkins Vocational and Applied Technology Education Act.* Madison: Wisconsin Technical College System Board, 1994. (ED 377 892)

The stated purpose of the Carl D. Perkins Vocational, Technical, and Applied Technology Act is to make the United States more competitive in the world economy by developing more fully the academic and occupational skills of all segments of the population. The Wisconsin Department of Public Instruction (DPI) has proposed to achieve this purpose by concentrating resources on promoting and developing tech-prep and youth apprenticeship programs in accordance with its school-to-work initiative. The Wisconsin Technical College System Board (WTCSB) has used its share of the federal funds to support activities that provide services for members of special populations, as well as for improving programs and services for all students. This 257-page document contains the 1994–96 two-year plan adopted by the WTCSB. The plan constitutes the basis for the operation and administration of the state's vocational education program under the Perkins Act. Also included are assessment and funding provisions, a state profile, DPI-WTCSB needs assessment, DPI-WTCSB proposed use of Perkins funding, DPI-WTCBS tech-prep provisions, DPI-WTCSB assurances and descriptions, and information on certification hearings, reviews, and responses.

Tech-Prep Programs

The articles in this section highlight tech-prep programs, which are a specific type of school-to-work program.

Falcone, L., and Mundhenk, R. (eds.). *The Tech-Prep Associate Degree Challenge: A Report of the Tech-Prep Roundtable.* AACC Special Reports No. 6. Washington, D.C.: American Association of Community Colleges, 1994. (ED 370 660)
     In the fall of 1993, a roundtable was held with leading tech-prep practitioners to discuss the direction tech-prep programs have taken since 1990 and emerging issues related to the implementation of tech-prep associate degree (TPAD) programs. This 91-page monograph describes tech-prep programs, provides recommendations for implementation, and reproduces six papers presented at the meeting. The first three sections provide introductory materials and a list of roundtable participants. Part Four reviews the history of the TPAD from the early 1980s and offers nineteen recommendations for implementing TPAD programs. Part Five presents a series of papers by roundtable participants. The monograph contains sixty references.

Newman, L. *A Comprehensive Tech-Prep Curriculum Model.* Oroville, Calif.: Butte College, 1994. (ED 369 448)
     The Butte College Tech-Prep Consortium (TPC), in Oroville, California, is a cooperative effort of secondary and postsecondary schools, local businesses, and community organizations to develop and implement tech-prep opportunities in the area. The TPC has developed a competency-based, comprehensive tech-prep curriculum model that is applicable to the differing needs of the institutions involved. Advantages of the model include its adaptability to long-range changes and school-to-work requirements and continuity with previous cooperative efforts such as 2 + 2 and 2 + 2 + 2 arrangements. The model establishes a balance between the academic core of sciences, communications, mathematics, and physics, technical and vocational preparation, and career development, focusing on developing students' critical thinking, team-

work, and other personal qualities. Diagrams of program organization and sample competency equivalencies are attached. Thirty-four pages.

Parnell, D. "The Tech-Prep Associate Degree Program Revisited." Paper presented at the Second Annual Conference on Workforce Training of the League for Innovation in the Community College, New Orleans, La., January 30– February 2, 1994. (ED 369 441)

Current education reform efforts show a lack of attention to the three out of four students currently in the educational system who are unlikely to ever earn baccalaureate degrees. The tech-prep associate degree (TPAD) program is aimed at preparing this neglected majority for the demands of a complex and shifting economy and improving teaching and learning. TPAD programs received funding under the Perkins Applied Technology and Vocational Education Act to provide planning and demonstration grants to consortia of high schools and community and technical colleges for development of four-year (grades 11–14) associate degree or certificate programs; provide comprehensive curricular links between high schools and community colleges, emphasizing occupationally specific programs; and combine knowing with doing in the teaching-learning process. Eight years later, the most successful TPAD efforts exhibited the following characteristics: cooperative partnerships among high school and community college personnel, regular involvement of employer and labor representatives, high expectations of students, and applied academics curricula to help students reach these expectations. Eleven pages.

The Effectiveness of School-to-Work Programs

These documents focus on the effectiveness of school-to-work programs and ways in which they can be evaluated.

Bragg, D. D., and Hamm, R. E. "The Opportunities for 'School-to-Work': A National Study of Work-Based Learning in U.S. Community Colleges." *Community College Journal*, 1995, *65*(7), 39–44.

This article examines findings from a two-year national study of work-based learning programs in community colleges. The authors indicate that community colleges, when provided with the requisite opportunity, resources, and support, can deliver valuable work-based learning experiences to students. The School-to-Work Opportunities Act of 1994 is described. The article features seventeen citations.

Grummon, P.T.H. "Evaluating Systemic Change in School-to-Work Initiatives." Paper presented at the Annual Meeting of the American Educational Research Association, New Orleans, April 1994. (ED 372 249)

A longitudinal study examined the factors affecting the long-term success of a midwestern tech-prep consortium consisting of one community college and four counties with a mix of rural, urban, and suburban communities. The study was designed to identify the effects of systematic change over time from the following perspectives: students' skill gains; how and what teachers teach; the broader school environment in which instruction occurs; district-level, parental, and business support for tech-prep programs; and the impact of state and federal policies on local-level tech-prep programming. The following data collection methods were used: review of historical documents; analysis of educational records; participant observation; field observation of business classrooms in a high school, comprehensive high school, vocational center, and community college; surveys; and interviews. Six months after the study had begun, a number of aspects of implementation of systematic change were identified. The thirteen-page article contains twenty references.

Maine State Department of Education. *State of Maine Annual Performance Report on Applied Technology Programs Funded Under the Carl D. Perkins Vocational and Applied Technology Act (P.L. 101-392). Program Year 1993–1994.* Augusta: Division of Applied Technology, Maine State Department of Education, 1994. (ED 380 672)

This 125-page report summarizes 1993–1994 program year developments in Maine's applied technology programs funded under the 1990 Carl D. Perkins Act. The first section highlights the following program activities: continued development of Maine's integrated school-to-work transition system, which allows secondary students to choose one of six career opportunity pathways as part of their individual opportunity plan; expansion of tech-prep and applied technology programs; adoption of a revised set of standards and measures for applied technology programs; and work toward creation of a Universal Student Information System. The program overview is followed by seventeen performance reports detailing 1993–1994 activities in the following areas: secondary, postsecondary, and adult occupational preparation programs; single parents, displaced homemakers, single pregnant women, and sex equity programs; programs for criminal offenders; programs for special populations; state leadership and professional development; community-based organization support; consumer and home economics education; tech-prep programs; and career guidance and counseling.

Stevens, D. W. *The School-to-Work Transition of High School and Community College Vocational Program Completers: 1990–1992.* EQW Working Papers WP27. Philadelphia: National Center on the Educational Quality of the Workforce, 1994. (ED 393 997)

The school-to-work transition of high school and community college vocational program completers in 1990–1992 was examined by analyzing administrative records and employment and earnings data of vocational program completers from state education agencies in Colorado, Florida, Missouri, and Washington. A consistently high percentage of vocational program completers at both the high school and postsecondary levels continued an uninterrupted affiliation with the same employer during the bridge period encompassing their last months in school and first few months after leaving school; however, substantial movement between employers during the first years after the former students left school was observed. Former students who continued with the same employer through the bridge period were consistently found to have higher earnings than their classmates while they were still in school, shortly after leaving school, and at the end of the postschool reference period. One hundred and fourteen pages.

MATTHEW BURSTEIN is user services coordinator for the ERIC Clearinghouse for Community Colleges in Los Angeles.

INDEX

ORDERING INFORMATION

NEW DIRECTIONS FOR COMMUNITY COLLEGES is a series of paperback books that provides expert assistance to help community colleges meet the challenges of their distinctive and expanding educational mission. Books in the series are published quarterly in Spring, Summer, Fall, and Winter and are available for purchase by subscription and individually.

SUBSCRIPTIONS cost $53.00 for individuals (a savings of 33 percent over single-copy prices) and $89.00 for institutions, agencies, and libraries. Please do not send institutional checks for personal subscriptions. Standing orders are accepted. Prices subject to change. (For subscriptions outside of North America, add $7.00 for shipping via surface mail or $25.00 for air mail. Orders *must be prepaid* in U.S. dollars by check drawn on a U.S. bank or charged to VISA, MasterCard, or American Express.)

SINGLE COPIES cost $20.00 plus shipping (see below) when payment accompanies order. California, New Jersey, New York, and Washington, D.C., residents please include appropriate sales tax. Canadian residents add GST and any local taxes. Billed orders will be charged shipping and handling. No billed shipments to post office boxes. (Orders from outside North America *must be prepaid* in U.S. dollars by check drawn on a U.S. bank or charged to VISA, MasterCard, or American Express.)

SHIPPING (SINGLE COPIES ONLY): $20.00 and under, add $3.50; to $50.00, add $4.50; to $75.00, add $5.50; to $100.00, add $6.50; to $150.00, add $7.50; over $150.00, add $8.50.

DISCOUNTS FOR QUANTITY ORDERS are available. Please write to the address below for information.

ALL ORDERS must include either the name of an individual or an official purchase order number. Please submit your order as follows:
   Subscriptions: specify series and year subscription is to begin
   Single copies: include individual title code (such as CC82)

MAIL ALL ORDERS TO:
   Jossey-Bass Publishers
   350 Sansome Street
   San Francisco, California 94104-1342

FOR SUBSCRIPTION SALES OUTSIDE OF THE UNITED STATES, contact any international subscription agency or Jossey-Bass directly.